Music Production & DJing for EDM: Everything You Need To Know To Become A World Famous EDM DJ & Music Producer

Copyright Notice

No part of this book may be reproduced or transmitted in any form whatsoever, electronic, or mechanical, including photocopying, recording, or by any information storage or retrieval system without expressed written, dated and signed permission from the author. All copyrights are reserved.

Disclaimer

Reasonable care has been taken to ensure that the information presented in this book is accurate. However, the reader should understand that the information provided does not constitute legal, medical or professional advice of any kind.

No Liability: this product is supplied "as is" and without warranties. All warranties, express or implied, are hereby disclaimed. Use of this product constitutes acceptance of the "No Liability" policy. If you do not agree with this policy, you are not permitted to use or distribute this product.

We shall not be liable for any losses or damages whatsoever (including, without limitation, consequential loss or damage) directly or indirectly arising from the use of this product.

Claim This Now

Music Business Skills for Musicians:

If you're in the music business, read on. Today you need to view yourself through the new rules of the music industry.

Those who play by them will succeed.

Gone are the old days where you would hope to get signed and then become a star (i.e., everything would be done for you).

Do you wonder why other artists are getting breaks and you are not?

Discover "How To Find Your Sound"

Find Out More

Swindali music coaching/Skype lessons.

Email djswindali@gmail.com for info and pricing.

Electronic Dance Music Production: The Advanced Guide On How to Produce Music for EDM Producers

INTRODUCTION

THE MAIN GENRES OF EDM

THE ELEMENTS
- THE KICK
- THE LEAD
  - The Best Synths For Making EDM Leads
  - Layering
- BASS
  - The Best Synths For Making EDM Bass
- DRUMS
  - Why Tuning Your Drums is Essential
  - Drum Programming
  - Tips and Tricks
- VOCALS
- FX
- EDM SONG CONSTRUCTION
  - All You Need to Know About Music Theory
- ARRANGEMENT
  - Intro
  - Breakdown
  - Buildup
  - Drop
  - Outro
- REMAKE: THE BEST WAY TO IMPROVE
- HOW TO REMIX
- MIXING EDM
- MASTERING
  - How to master EDM with iZotope Ozone
- DIGITAL AUDIO WORK STATION (DAW)
  - Ableton Live

- FL Studio
- Logic Pro X
- Steinberg Cubase
- Reason

MUST HAVE PLUGINS
VIRTUAL STUDIO INSTRUMENTS
PLUG INS
- Analyzers
- Delay
- Distortion
- Dynamics
- Effects
- Filters
- Misc
- Musical
- Reverb
- Stereo Imaging
- Vocals

GET SIGNED
- Branding
- Contacting Labels
  - Tips

CONCLUSION

BONUS: GHOST PRODUCING

BONUS: 18 THINGS EVERY EDM PRODUCER NEEDS TO SUCCEED

INTRODUCTION

Welcome to *Electronic Dance Music Production: The Advanced Guide On How to Produce Music for EDM Producers.* Your about discover what it takes to make an EDM song from idea, to finished song, to getting signed and more. Whether your a beginner or a more experienced producer your going to find value from this book.

When you think of EDM you will probably imagine big festivals, huge anthems and epic productions. All of that might well seem a million miles away from what you believe is possible for yourself. But let me tell you what those big name DJs do is not all that different from what most bedroom producers do. That is all easily achievable with the right knowledge, techniques and a few tools. The biggest difference between you and the big stars is in ideas and quality. Skillset, knowledge and tools are almost the same.

All you need to know and more will be covered in this book. From the knowledge of music to getting inspired and creating an epic EDM song. I'm even going to show the steps to get that song signed and out there for the world to hear.

Imagine the possibilities of having your song signed to a major label.

It's no secret that the top DJ's got there because of the music they make. You could be there too. Mainstage Ultra Music Festival, playing in clubs worldwide and getting your songs heard. Or maybe you just want to learn how to make an EDM track from start to finish. There are so many possibilites. All of that will be covered and much more.

The flow of this book will begin with an outline of EDM, then it will focus on the journey of a song from concept to production, mixing, mastering and then how to get it out there. You can decide to go through this chapter by chapter or you can jump straight to the parts that interest you the most. Remember that learning something takes repetition so always come back and refresh your knowledge. Now let's get started producing EDM.

THE MAIN GENRES OF EDM

EDM is a broad way of defining dance music. As a whole it encompasses music that is suited for the dance floor. Within that umbrella genre there are many more genres that vary massively from each other. Let's take a look at some of the most popular ones. This will give you a clearer picture of what to expect when producing within that genre. You can also check out how difficult each genre is to produce within the descriptions. Don't be put off by that though, learning curves can be quite steep at the start but once you climb them your flying.

*higher scores mean it is more easy to produce.

Big Room: (126 - 130 BPM)
Big room is one of the most popular sub genres of electro house music and EDM. It was popularized by the likes of artists such as Hardwell, Martin Garrix, KSHMR and R3hab.

The music is very formulaic and one of the easiest to produce. All tracks will include a long techno style build up that goes into a big drop with a 4/4 hard, bass thumping kick. Minimal musical elements, synths and percussion usually fill in space but most of the room is left for a huge kick.

*Difficulty to produce: 8/10

Drum and Bass: (160 - 180 BPM)
Drum and bass also known as D'n'B, is a subgenre of EDM which was born in the UK jungle and rave movements during

the early 90s. Fast breakbeats, with big bass lines, samples, and synths characterize the genre.

A major influence on D'n'B comes from the Jamaican dub and reggae sound. It also incorporates a number of scenes and styles, from highly electronic, industrial sounds the jazz-influenced end of the spectrum. From its UK roots, the style has gained worldwide recognition and has influenced many other genres.

Difficulty to produce: 4/10

Dubstep: (140 - 155 BPM)

Dubstep is a subgenre of EDM that originated in London. It is generally characterized by syncopated rhythmic patterns and strong sub bass lines. The drums of Dubstep tend to be simple one shot kicks and snares with some hats. This simplicity makes a nice contrast for the wobbly, complex basslines.

Difficulty to produce: 3/10

Electro House: (126 - 130 BPM)
Electro house is a subgenre of house music that is distinguished by heavy basslines that are usually creating with lots of distortion and automation. In addition to a large bass drum in a 4/4 pattern. As with Dubstep the drums are usually simple to contrast complex basslines. It can also include melodic elements, samples and synth work. Generally the tempo falls around 130 BPM.

Difficulty to produce: 3/10

Future Bass: (145 - 160 BPM)
Future bass is a sub genre of electronic dance music that features elements of Trap music and is characterized by modulated synthesizer bass sounds. Sounds are modulated with automation or LFO's to create choppy effects. Arpeggio chords, vocal chops and vocoders are also popular in the genre. More mainstream Future bass music uses supersaw chords, whilst underground sounds experiment more with other sounds.

Difficulty to produce: 2/10

Hardstyle: (150 - 160 BPM)
Hardstyle is takes characteristics from hardcore and techno. Typically consists of a distorted, hard sounding kick drum. Multiple layers are combined to create a big and lead style kick. Hardstyle also utilises harsh and distorted synths, detuned and distorted sounds accompanying the main instruments.

Hardstyle has influenced many other styles of EDM, Most notably Big Room. This shares similarities with hardstyle such structure, rhythm and pitched kicks.

Difficulty to produce: 6/10

Psytrance:(135 - 150 BPM)
Psytrance also known as psychedelic trance or psy is a subgenre of trance music. Psytrance is easily recognizable with its use of a strong bass beat that usually occurs throughout the whole song. This is interlaced between the kicks on a fast and varying rhythm that might be in triplet or standard form.

Typically it falls between the 135 to 150 BPM range and is usually faster than trance. The layouts are usually long, sometimes well over ten minutes. These are progressive with various elements and layers coming in at regular intervals and leading to breakdowns.

The mood can vary from minimal to progressive, chill and dancefloor.

Difficulty to produce: 7/10

Trap: (140 - 160 BPM)
Trap is an amalgamation of dubstep and classic trap hip hop. As a subgenre it emerged around 2012. It is categorized by the use of 808 basslines, big subs and some minimal melodic elements. The BPM of a typical trap beat is around 140 to 160 BPM. Typically has strong bass drops and hard sounds.

Difficulty to produce: 5/10

THE ELEMENTS

When your producing EDM regardless of sub genre there are going to be some consistent elements that appear. Let's take a look at how to create and work with those.

THE KICK

In EDM the kick is the most important element. Remember kick sounds are dependent on the genre. Some things works well for different genres. For example big room favours bigger kicks whilst electro house goes with smaller kicks.

Using samples is the best solution for getting great sounding kicks, fast. These can be found within sample packs or on Splice which hosts a huge library containing billions of amazing samples.

Use my invite: https://splice.com/vip/Tommyswin

Every kick sample can essentially be cut into three different sections.

Tic/click: This is the transient starting sound. Usually it's going to be around five ten milliseconds long and contains quick attack, high frequency content. In essence this is what allows the kick to kind of jump out of the mix. Without the tick it will be very hard to hear any kick. Especially on speakers that are smaller such as headphones, laptop speakers and so on.

Body: Next section, will be anywhere from a hundred to one hundred and fifty milliseconds. This is where you start to move away from the high frequency content of the tick into the kind of low mids. In essence it's the punch and is what gives the kick energy.

Tail: The last section is where you can start to perceive the pitch of a kick. The tail can be as long short as you want. The longer it is, the more easily it will be to tell the keys. 808 Kicks usually have quite long tails and are often used as a bassline playing a melody.

Understanding how these sections work will make mixing and creating kicks a lot easier and quicker because you will be making informed decisions. Let's say you take your kick to a smaller speaker environment such as your car laptop speakers and you can't hear it. That may mean that your kick tick isn't strong enough. Or it might mean that your punch is too short or it has too much low frequency content. Tweaking the different sections can help to fix things. If all else fails try a new sample.

Tune Your Kicks
To make sure your kicks work the best with your songs always tune them to the root note of the key of your song. Now if you like having kicks that are in perfect tune with your song then there are plugins which will create kicks such as, Sonic Academy kick. Otherwise your going to be using a sample of which you will need to know the key.

To determine the key of the sample you can use a free plugin named Span by Voxengo. This is an analysing plugin which will display the frequency and key of an input sound. The way to identify key is to look for where the waveform peaks a little bit higher on the analyzer screen. Press play and then scroll over to the peak amplitude. Then you will see the key reading at the bottom of the screen.

Once you know the key of a kick you can change it as you wish. Normally it's best to stick within the required key or within a range of two semitones. If you want to pitch kicks up or down you can load them into any sampler and transpose them up or down. Samplers are also great for loading multiple samples and then drawing them out in midi. Another way to pitch your samples is to use the built in tools of your DAW or plug ins such as soundshifter from Waves.

Best Frequencies to EQ a Kick
There are some magic frequencies for kick drums which work pretty well. For the best results use a parametric EQ. Using this you can set a wide of narrow Q band to add or remove frequencies. Here are some useful frequencies to consider with your kicks.

100 to 200 Hertz: Kicks consist of dominant low frequencies. In some instances the kick drum might low frequency impact. The Waves Renaissance bass can come in here. It sounds great it's easy to use and you'll get fast results. You can also boost in this frequency range for good results. Always high pass the very lowest frequencies (below 30 HZ) since these usually clip limiters and cause distortion.

200-500 Hz: Boxy sound. Generally something we don't want. Many kicks have a lot of energy here so we usually have to take it out a little bit.

Around to 2 KHZ: The attack / click of the sound. Enhancing this helps to to define the kick more clearly. Many people assume kicks are all about bass but the mids are very important for rhythm. If your song has a fast rhythm you will benefit from short kicks with well defined mids.

THE LEAD

The real secret to a great lead is the melody. A melody is by definition monophonic which means that it is one voice without any chords. A melody can be characterized by four elements:

- **Contour**

A contour can be thought of as a line that ascends, descends, dips or arches. Different contours evoke different emotions and how they are used is down to preference.

- **Range**

The range of a melody is the distance between it's highest and lowest note. Most EDM melodies work well on a smaller range (half to full octave) because EDM is dependent on sounding big and powerful. Bigger ranges mean shifting in pitches which weakens sounds as they move from the root note. Just remember that narrower ranges are less musical. Focus on smaller ranges for the drop and wider ranges for melodic breakdowns.

- **Intervals**

Melodies always use more than one note and so there will always be at least one melodic interval. Think of this as the blueprint and it will help you create alterations for different parts of your melody. Does the melody jump down to certain notes or move to them incrementally?

- **Structure**

Melodies are based on a structure too. You can have different sections of your melody. That could be call and response, up and down, etc.

- **Scales**

Scales form melodies and there are numerous types:
- Modal: Variable patterns of major/minor scale.
- Major and minor: The majority of Western music.
- Chromatic: All twelve notes.
- Pentatonic Scale: 5-note scale. Often used in blues and rock.
- There are others, but those are irrelevant to EDM production.

In EDM with a little theory and structure you can create a melody more quickly and easily. Try these five steps.

1. Scale

Work with a scale and this limits the amount of notes you can use. EDM producers usually work with one scale most of the time. F Minor is particularly popular. Learning and sticking to a scale will help you to know which notes will work.

2. Rhythm

After deciding on a scale you need a rhythm for your melody. A bunch of notes is nothing but with a simple rhythm a melody is born. You can tap out a rhythm or try some percussion to map the rhythm out.

3. Contour

Once the rhythm is locked in, it's time to outline the melody. This is where you get creative and imagine where the note falls. Is it up, down or the same? Follow your vision.

4. Sound

If you have a great melody it will sound amazing with pretty much any instrument. Spend time getting that right with basic sounds and then develop the sound design. It's better to do that first otherwise your wasting time trying to turn something average into something spectacular. Start with good sources. Later on you might wish to move and vary notes as you please.

If you get stuck try using silence, changing instruments, shifting octaves or moving notes around. Try to get a decent four to eight bar melody. Take inspiration from other music and even use MIDI files.

The Best Synths For Making EDM Leads

Nowadays there are so many synths available to make leads with. The best option is to find one that you feel comfortable with and can easily get great results with. Results won't come instantly until you master the synth. So for starters, try to use less instead of spreading your skills across a bunch of different synths. To help you decide, let's take a look at three of the best currently on the market. These are used by some of the top producers in the EDM world.

Sylenth

Sylenth is a legend and has been around since 2007. But it has continued to develop and has stood the test of time with it's huge array of soundbanks and amazing sonics. Every EDM producer should have it installed.

It is capable of making almost any sound from bass, pads, percussion and more. But the real highlight is how good it is at making EDM leads.

- Spec: Subtractive synthesizer with four oscillators, two filters, two envelopes, and two LFOS.
- Artists: Afrojack, Hardwell, Avicii, Skrillex, The Chainsmokers and more…
- https://www.lennardigital.com/sylenth1/

Serum

Serum is the EDM synth to have and right now is one of the most popular synthesizers on the market. It is a beast at making EDM leads and hosts hundreds of soundbanks plus a library full of high quality presets. Excels at sounds for Dubstep, Trap and Future Bass. It's unlimited LFO's are great for making hard and interesting leads. Add this to your EDM arsenal.

- Spec: Wavetable Synthesizer with three envelopes, unlimited LFOS, two Filters, ten built in effects, and thousands of wavetables.
- Artists: Dyro, Deadmau5, Morgan Page, DJ Snake, Skrillex and more...
- https://xferrecords.com/products/serum

Spire

A hidden gem that is a strong contender for making the best EDM leads. Easy to use with a plethora of customizable presets. Great for trance and progressive sounds with lush textures or Big Room leads. Anthems sound great with this. Offers almost everything as Sylenth and Serum but in a different package that should be part of your EDM production arsenal.

- Spec: A subtractive, wavetable, FM and AM Synthesizer with two Filters, and standard modulations.

- Artists: Hardwell, Armin Van Buuren, Dimitri Vegas & Like Mike and more…
- https://www.reveal-sound.com/

Samples
Making lead sounds with synths can be a long and arduous task. If you struggle with it you can always make use of samples. Splice is a great resource.

https://splice.com/vip/Tommyswin

You can browse the library for synth sounds as one note samples. Load the samples into a sampler such as Kontakt or the built in sampler of your DAW. You can then play in your lead melody and have that sample play it. Amazing sounding results almost instantly!

Layering
Want to make huge leads? If you are looking to create epic leads then layering multiple synths is the way to go. The trick to layering synths is in knowing what type of synths to layer together. For that to work you need to choose sounds that will compliment each other and sound great as one.

The first sound you use should be a simple synth sound and usually that would be in mono. This works great on big sound systems so having it as your base sound is perfect. The init sound in Sylenth is a great starting point. If your melody sounds good with basic sounds then you're onto a winning track because its then going to sound amazing when you add in all the layers and effects processing.

Normally layers won't sound great on their own so avoid using the solo button. The next layer to add can be a nice wide lead to fill out the stereo field. Then you will have a good mix of mono and stereo for making a huge full lead. You can keep adding more layers but just be conscious of having a purpose for them. A trick you can use with the layering is to have them dropping in and out. This can work really well with progressive EDM styles.

Want more distortion? Add a distorted layer. Want more realness? Add some live world instruments. Just make sure they all compliment each other. You can EQ layers individually to remove any unwanted or clashing frequencies or even add effects processing as you please. It's a good practice to send all those layers to a bus so they can all be controlled as one. Finally add some master effects such as reverb, compression and so on. Sidechaining on the leads helps to make them fit in more with the kick.

BASS

Bass is without a doubt at the core of EDM music. It might be subtle or extremely exaggerated but regardless without it EDM would sound dead. In layman's terms it is the low pitched instrumental part of a song. In some cases such as with trap it might be an 808 kick drum. In other cases it might be lower register of an instrument or a synthesizer.

Without a good bass line to back your drop, your song won't get to the next level. Great basslines consist of an awesome sound and a great groove. Here are some tips to make your bass lines sound awesome. You can also apply some of the tips you learned to create melodies.

- **Match the bassline with the kick**. A good relation between these will provide a strong foundation for the track. Adding in other instruments later will be a breeze.
- **Get inspired**. Listen to other songs how does the bass sound, what is it's rhythm? Don't be afraid to copy a little because it will help your bass lines sound great and get you inspired. Just make sure you add in some originality.
- **Layer**. Again this will help you basslines become much fuller, fatter and bigger. Most sounds on their own are not enough. You can even add in some modulated layers to make your bass sound super interesting. Use tools such as compression and distortion to gel the layers together.
- **Slide notes**. This will create nice transitions between notes. Almost all synthesizers come with the portamento/legato function that can be adjusted to

make notes slide into each other. This will work wonders on basslines.
- ***Harmonizing***. Most bass lines follow the root notes of the chords played by other instruments. Try changing the bass notes to others that are in harmony with your chords and you will get a whole new flavor of bass.
- ***Bouncy***. If the rhythm sounds good but it's boring, make it bouncy. Simply putting certain notes up an octave and elongating some of them will give you a more bouncy and interesting bass line. Remember to turn on the legato as with sliding technique.

The Best Synths For Making EDM Bass

Now when it comes to the sound of the bass your going to need a solid, reliable synth. You could go with bass guitars or pianos on the low riff but that's less common in EDM. Here are some of the best virtual instruments for bass.

Novation Bass Station
If you're looking for warm, fat and dirty basslines then Bass Station will deliver. It's two distinct analogue filter types offer massive variation in sonic possibilities. The sounds can be strong or soft as you wish. Crank the distortion for more hardness or tweek the filters to soften. Comes with sixty four diverse patches to get you started.

- Spec: Analogue Monosynth emulation with two oscillators and one sub oscillator.
- Artists: Soul Clap, Brohug, Vini Vici and more…
- https://novationmusic.com/synths/bass-station-ii

Native Instruments Massive

Massive is a hugely popular synth with EDM producers. Instead of taking direct inspiration from vintage hardware, Massive uses a combination of wavetable synthesis technology and a simple drag-and-drop interface for programming. It practically gave birth to dubstep with its wobbly bass lines and has gone onto be a go to synth for future house and bass house producers. Great at creating traditional analogue style tones to complex evolving sounds.

- Spec: Wavetable Synthesizer with multiple envelopes, LFOS, two Filters, built in effects, and thousands of wavetables.
- Artists: Sub Focus, Knife Party, Dannic, Swedish House Mafia and more…
- https://www.native-instruments.com/en/products/komplete/synths/massive/

Rob Papen SubBoomBass
This is one of EDM basses best kept secrets. The design might scream "80s", but inside is a modern and powerful sound engine. In addition the standard sine, square, saw and triangle waveforms are many sampled waveforms for adding texture to your bass. The result is an organic-sounding and powerful bass plug-in. Comes with a huge bank of great presets.

- Spec: Dual Oscillator Synthesizer with envelopes, LFOS and sequencer
- Artists: Junkie XL, DJ Khaled, DJ Mustard and more…
- https://www.robpapen.com/subboombass.html

DRUMS

EDM is built on its drums which entice people to dance. A bad beat will ruin a song.

Why Tuning Your Drums is Essential
Tuning your drum and percussion parts is essential to achieving a great song. Like all other instruments, the drums need to be in the same key as the song.

Use a key and frequency chart to identify specific notes. This will help you identify the key for your individual drum hits. For example, if you have a song in the key of A, it would sound best to boost at frequency ranges matching the A note. The frequency note chart will show you all those ranges for each of the notes across the spectrum. Use other notes in the same key to give your drum hits different character and help them stand out. Many EDM producers tune their snares up a fifth from the root note.

Everyone has their own unique mixing process music. Depending on the music style we have our default ways that define us. A big influence on mixing is how we use Equalizers (EQ) for different instruments. EQ is a tool used to enhance or remove frequencies from sounds. Another way to use an EQ is to tune drum hits so that they match the key of your song. Use a tuner whilst EQ'ing. When applied to a channel a tuner will identify what key your drum hit is. If it's out of key, you can shift your EQ settings until it matches the right key. Alternatively you can use a frequency shifter to tweek the specific part without losing any clarity or tonality.

Drum Programming

Drum programming is the process of composing with drums. Instead of playing drums live you are actually drawing them out in a sequence. This is different drum synthesis since you are not actually creating the sounds. Instead you're using drum samples. As you can imagine this can take a while because you have to pick the right samples, layer and then construct sequences.

Fundamentally drum programming is easy. Anyone can create a basic kick-hat-snare drum pattern. But when you go deeper and want to create more interesting, complex and great sounding drums it becomes more complicated. Learning is an ongoing journey. You can always learn from other songs. Analyze them, consider the different elements and what makes them good. Be an active listener and take notes.

Great drums begin with sourcing the best samples. With better samples, less work will be required. Then you won't need to rely on layering multiple hits together. Sometimes if all that is needed is one hit then that's fine. Layering drums can be a complicated task and often it's best to choose just one good sample.

There really is no secret method or technique for finding great samples, it's all about trusting your ears. Developing your listening skills is critical to becoming better at that. Unfortunately out there are many low quality samples. If you're considering to buy a sample pack download a demo first. This way you can test out the samples first. Truthfully you will only need a few great samples anything more and you'll waste time searching for the perfect sample. Don't waste time searching. Choose the one that works, and then process it so it becomes perfect. One of the best websites for samples is [Splice](). It's a paid monthly service that offers you millions of sounds for all EDM genres.

Add Interest and Variation to Your Drums
Repeating the same drum loop for sixteen bars gets boring really quick. You do need the main drum loop but you also should make it more interesting.

Try the following techniques
- Every two bars, introduce a new drum hit
- Every four bars, introduce a new drum hit that's stronger or louder
- Every eight bars create a drum fill or roll

These techniques aren't the only ones you can try. Experiment and it will turn a boring loop into an interesting one. Analyze the drums in your favorite EDM and apply it to your productions.

In addition you can add swing to your drums to give them a natural feeling. This is essentially small variations in velocity and time to enhance the groove and rhythm. You can apply this manually to individual hits, changing velocity, timing and so on or in some DAWs they have a setting that you can apply in intensity. This will make your drums more funky and exciting. Experiment with it.

Big Room
Big room is pure simplicity when it comes to drum programming. It's designed for festivals and clubs, not for home listening. Typically it will have a sub bass, distorted kick tuned to the root note of the song. Often this is combined with a clap that has reverb added to it which is sidechained with

the kick. Also you will often have a high passed ride cymbal on the top. Sometimes you will hear some percussion playing on off beats. Every eight or sixteen bars the patterns will have a fill. When selecting samples choose big and simple hits.

Drum and Bass
Drum and bass is fast and is one of the hardest genres to make drums for. Having the snare right is an important thing to get right. Get this right and the foundation is solid. Then you want a hard hitting tuned kick. The next thing is to layer in many different hi hats and breakbeats to fill up the drums. Create diversity and interest with new drums every so often then progressing into fills and rolls every sixteen bars.

Dubstep
Drums in dubstep are there to support the bassline and are often very simple. Often they will consist of a very strong kick and snare combined with shuffle style hi hats which break up monotony. All are of course tuned to the key of the song. Remember to tune your snare up a 5th for diversity. Add in some subtle percussion to create more interest. Every so often add in some new hits or even modulate the snare by making it shorter, longer or changing pitch and so on.

Electro House
Electro house drums are often using very simple patterns. In most cases it's simply just a kick, snare and hihat. The purpose of simplicity is usually to contrast with the complex arrangements of bass and synths. Generally the drums sound dirty and rock style. Select samples that have a rough characteristic. Rolls and fills are less common in elector house in some cases there will be a pause and some fx take their place.

Future Bass and Trap
Drums in Future Bass and Trap are quite similar. The drums are almost always consisting of a kick drum, snare, and hi-hats. Kicks are usually coming from a tuned 808 sample to the root note of the song. Often this will also play some kind of a melody. Then the snare would probably be pitched a 5th up from the root. Hi-Hats are very important to the character of trap. Percussion sounds in Trap are quite experimental and will often include unique sounds to give more character. Normally Future Bass songs have more real world sounding drums. You can get really creative with the variations, add in breaks or new hits as you please. Just make sure to keep the rest of the song in mind and help the track as a whole.

Hardstyle
This is very similar to the simplicity and arrangement of Big Room. The main difference is obviously the tempo but going further Hardstyle is actually even more minimal. Often the only drum programming is the kick. This is left alone because it is the focal point. Hardstyle kicks are multiple layers or resampled and distorted kicks to create a huge monster of a sound that fills the whole spectrum. This would be tuned to the root note and usually play a melody. Fills take the place of any areas where the kick doesn't play. Usually every sixteen bars or so.

Psytrance
Psytrance is very kick driven. Short and low frequency full sounding kicks work well here. They play a 4/4 beat and are usually supported by some light percussion or hi hats. You have to keep things minimal but full sounding with Psytrance otherwise you move away from the character of the genre.

Tips

- Make samples fit by applying Attack, Decay, Sustain, Release (ADSR)
- Adding effects won't improve a bad sample
- Apply swing for complexity and a human feel
- Keep it simple. Always make sure you have a reason to add new samples
- Create interest through variation. Vary your drums every eight to sixteen bars
- Practice. Remake some of your favourite tracks.
- Compliment the track and make space for the instruments.

VOCALS

Some of the biggest EDM songs feature vocals. Vocals capture your heart, mind and emotions. Having the vocals right is going to make EDM production awesome. With that said here are some fundamentals to achieving great vocals. Remember to add on a healthy dose of, experimentation, inspiration, and creativity.

Processing EDM Vocals is one of the most important skills a producer can develop. At the start you need to make sure your vocals are great without any processing. The number one way to achieve this is to find a good singer. Someone with experience and talent is going to give you a great vocal performance. Maybe you have a song idea you can send them. Or it could be a cover, your own lyrics or maybe their ideas. Ideally find someone who is creatively sharing your mindset. Harmonious working relationships will produce great results.

Now the singer doesn't really need to have a big vocal range but some experience is required. Ideally, you should find someone who fits your song and has an original vocal character. Screening for these attributes will ensure a great vocal performance.

Once you have your vocalist it's time to get into the technicalities. First of all select the right microphone. Condenser microphones are generally more suitable for recording vocals because of their sensitivity to high frequency detail. However dynamic microphones will work fine if your budget is lower. Famous artists have achieved great results with both. Make sure you set the microphone up at a distance that captures them effectively. Not too close but not too far. Finally add on a pop shield to attenuate plosive sounds.

Avoid any effects processing for now. EDM songs usually have heavily process vocals but all that should be saved for later on. If you do it now you can't undo it so it's better to capture a raw and well recorded vocal. You don't even need compression or limiting going in. Just make sure you use a good quality recording interface, cables and microphone. Save the effects for later.

Capture the best performance. Remember that the one thing above all else is to record the greatest vocals possible. Your job is to make sure the singer delivers their best performance. Make sure they are comfortable, that their monitor feed is at the right level and even small things such as if they need water or a short rest. Some of the best vocal recordings happen on first takes so be focused on the results and don't waste time if you get the result early on. If things aren't working out then take a short break.

Once you have recorded a good vocal performance you can begin to clean things up. Often there will be some low level noise on recordings. You can use a noise reduction plug-in to clean that. Have the settings light so that you aren't muting out parts. If there are long empty sections you can trim out those. But keep it natural and retain any breathing because this will help to maintain the natural vocal characteristics.

The next thing to clean up is everything below 100 HZ as that is likely rumble and not part of the vocal. Apply a simple high pass filter set at 100 HZ here. Once we have done this it's time to remove any unwanted resonating frequencies. These usually occur in very small rooms. The way to find them is by using an EQ with high Q band set and then sweeping it across the spectrum to listen for any areas that jump out. Once you find those all you need to do is then reduce the gain where you found them and that will be all for the cleaning portion.

It's time to start beefing it up. EDM vocals need to sound strong and clear. Compression will help to achieve that because a singer will never deliver a performance where their voice is loud all the time. This is where compression comes in by making the dynamic range of the vocal smaller. However compression must be used carefully because you don't want to take the life out of a vocal. Too much and it will result in a dead sound.

Adjust the threshold to catch the sound and the ratio to control how much to compress. Next, have the attack set so that the first transients keep their punchiness. Then again tweek the threshold and ratio controls as preferred. The result will be a more consistent vocal that will stand out in the mix. Also, De-ess your vocals to get rid of high frequency sibilant sounds and help make the vocal shine through the mix. Waves have some great presets adjusted for male and female singers.

The last step is to polish the vocals. Apply reverb, delay, and all the effects that make vocals sound amazing and powerful. First up add a little bit of warmer or saturation to warm up the vocals. Next use a simple delay to add a bit of a delay effect to make them sound more wide. After this apply a reverb to the vocal via a return. Using a return will maintain the clarity of the vocal and keep the effects clean. A return can be created in every DAW. Normally you just click send to a group. The best reverb for EDM vocals is a Hall style. However you can always flick between presets and then adjust the one you like.

When mixing your vocals make alternate mixes. Try creating three mixes:

- One where you feel the vocal should be
- One more upfront
- One pulled back

Chances are, one of these will be right. In addition make sure you mix the vocals in the rest of the mix. Avoid mixing in isolation because this will sound different to how it will sound in the mix. Mixing decisions should always be done within the mix of the whole song. Only solo the vocals in order to remove problematic frequencies or to fine tune.

This is just one way of mixing vocals. It's up to you to experiment and find unique ways to be more creative. Come up with your own ways of vocal processing and develop your sound.

FX

Add in some FX sounds to make your tracks sound more interesting. Maybe your song feels a bit empty. Trust me and add some FX. They will make all the difference. Get creative here and follow your intuition. To help you here are some of the most commonly used FX.

- **Atmospherics**

These are light and ethereal sounds with lots of ambience. Work great for intros or maybe in the background of more emotionally driven music. Create your own with simple or layered sounds that have lots of reverb on.

- **Background**

It's great to have some long sustained and evolving sounds going on in the background of an intro or drop. This keeps the listener hooked in. Try some tuned effects here to stick with the key.

- **Downers**

Whenever you come to a breakdown or build up it's a good idea to use a downer. This is simply a long sound pitched to the root note of the song that then glides down in pitch. Typically this will be a sub or low bass sound. Creates a great atmospheric effect.

- **Fills**

These are normally sixteen to one bar drum rolls but they could be things such as short bass notes that roll down the scale or anything your imagination can conceive. Place these every sixteen bars or more to break things up, introduce new sections and keep it interesting.

- **Impacts**

Use these with your downers or on their own. They are loud fast attack sounds with a long sustain and release. Snare drums and impact sounds with reverb work well here.

- **Lazers**

High pitched lfo sounds that work really well over the top of bass heavy music or breakdowns. They work really well when you introduce an important new section of your song such as a breakdown or drop.

- **Make Your Own**

Get creative. Buy yourself a microphone and use household objects your voice or anything else you think would be cool to record. Add it to your songs and make them original.

- **Risers**

The highlight of an EDM banger. When it comes to building up to a huge drop a riser is going to make sure the damage is done well. Take a long sound and pitch it up slowly or quickly over a whole octave or two. Always use risers in the key of your song.

- **Rolls**

Similar to fills but would only be one drum hit or sound repeated and speeding up. Great for going into drops.

- **Stabs**

Sounds with a fast attack and long release. Often a staccato horn sound is used, this is the case in 80% of trap. These can be a feature at the front or work well in the background. Always make sure they are in key.

- **Sweeps**

Can be long or short depending on how dramatic you want the effect to be. Use them to transition between sections of a song. Reversed cymbals or white noise work well as sweeps.

- **Tonal FX**

Anything that has strong resonant peak in the key of your song. These are great as atmospherics or can even be a main feature.

- **Vocal Samples**

If your song has vocals then it can be a great idea to create some vocal FX from the main hook. You could do some kind of pitched drops such as DJ Snake does or maybe just resample the vocals as atmospherics. Get creative and follow your imagination.

EDM SONG CONSTRUCTION

All You Need to Know About Music Theory

When you start out producing your going to hear about key a lot. So what is a key? Musically speaking key is the name given to a group of musical notes that will sound good when used together. When you use the notes within a particular key your songs will probably sound good. The first or lowest note in the key gives it the name. This is commonly referred to as the root or tonic note.

There are major keys and there are minor keys. In the simplest of terms. Major keys sound happy, and minor keys sound sad. The differences in these keys are in the intervals between each of the notes in the scale. Intervals consist of whole steps and half steps. The smallest interval between each note is half-step which is the equivalent of a semitone. You can identify all the notes of any key by counting the intervals from the root note. All major and minor keys are based on configurations of intervals.

- **Major Key**

Root Note (or Tonic) --> 2 (half-steps) --> 2 --> 1 --> 2 --> 2 --> 2 --> 1

- **Minor Key**

Root Note --> 2 (half-steps) --> 1 --> 2 --> 2 --> 1 --> 2 --> 2

The easiest way to know both is to consider the keys of C Minor and A Major. Both use the same notes (all the white keys) but use the intervals of major or minor respectively. So if you want to write in a particular major or minor key you can draw out all the notes used in either C Minor or A Major and then shift the root note to the key you wish to use. Alternatively you can just count the intervals using the above guides.

There are many other keys and scales too and there is much more to theory than this but for now this is the most important. Play and experiment with writing in different keys. This should help you to quickly and easily build your EDM tracks in key. It doesn't matter which genre you choose because it will work just as well for Drum and Bass as it will for House, Trap, Dubstep and so on.

Chords
The core of a song are the melody and chords. You don't need to be an expert in Music Theory to compose chords for your songs. As we now know every song is in a specific key and all of the other chords will revolve around it. For example a song could be in the key of C Major which uses all the white keys on a piano roll. Each one of the notes can be given a number which you will often see represented by Roman numerals.

Imagine chords like the building blocks of a story. Some will sound happy, some sad, some exciting, some relaxing and so on. Your job is to arrange these in a way that evokes the emotion you want. In a song the way chords move from one to the next is called a chord progression. The chords can evoke different feelings and there are many ways to combine chords. To start building a chord progression pick a key you like. Have a clear start and finish in mind when writing a chord progression. There also needs to be a degree of emotional development and movement which comes from using different chord progressions. Alternatively you could use the same chord progression but with a different melody.

EDM songs usually feature simple chord progressions that are easy to memorize. Often those will be only two to three chords. The foundation of EDM is usually simple but the complexity comes in arranging or sound design. A great way to start a song is to find a midi file of a chord progression you like or if you feel confident enough recreate it. Then focus on the sound design and different variations to make it sound your own. Here are some chords commonly found in EDM.

Triad Chord
A chord is generally when three or different keys are played at the same time. These are based on scales. The most common chord is a triad consisting of three keys, the first, the third and the fifth note of the scale. A triad is made up of a root, a third, and a fifth. Just count up the scale (including the root note) For example:

- C Major Triad Chord: **C, E, G**
- A Major Triad Chord: **A, C#, E**

Triads are the most common chords and you will hear many variations of them. You can switch the order of the notes of a chord from low to high to high to low. For example in C major you can put the C on top so that E becomes the lowest note and the G is in the middle. This is called "inversion".

Minor Chord
The next most common and easy to create chord is a minor. This is similar to the major except the third not is dropped by one half step. This gives it a sad emotional feeling. For example:

- C Minor Chord: **C, D#, G**
- A Minor Chord: **A, C, E**

Diminished Chords

Diminished chords can be used to add tension and a dissonant sound to your music. They are built by adding a minor third and a tritone above the root note. A tritone can be found by counting six semitones from the root note. Whilst a minor third can be found by counting three semitones from the root note. For example:

- C Diminished Chord: **C, D#, F#**
- A Diminished Chord: **A, C, D#**

Suspended Fourth

Suspended Fourth chords create a proud and strong emotion. These can be created by using the root, fourth and fifth note of the scale. For example

- C Suspended Fourth: **C, F, G**
- A Suspended Fourth: **A, D, E**

Major Sixth

Major Sixth chords use four notes to create a triumphant and strong emotion. Works well as a climax. These can be created by using the root, third, fifth and sixth note of the scale. For example:

- C Major Sixth: **C, E, G, A**
- A Major Sixth: **A, C#, E, F#**

Major Seventh Chord:

Nostalgic sounding chord that is created by using the root, third, fifth and seventh note of the scale. For example:

- C Major Seventh: **C, E, G, B**
- A Major Seventh: **A, C#, E, G#**

Dominant Seventh:
Expectant sounding chord that consists of a major third, perfect fifth, and minor seventh above a root. For example:

- C Dominant Seventh: **C, E, G, B#**
- A Dominant Seventh: **A, C#, E, G#**

Ninth Chords and More:
You can even go as far as using five notes in your chords or more. Just add notes on the top of your chords and experiment with sounds. Practice, trust your ears and go with what sounds best.

Try downloading some MIDI files of your favourite songs which will include all the notes of the song. You can use these to look at how the songs are put together and how all the notes work. This will give you a great understanding of music theory or perhaps even a song starter.

ARRANGEMENT

Most songs begin as loops. The hard part is taking a loop and turning it into a song. Many great loops with the potential to be great songs get stuck at the loop phase because of too much focus on perfection. It can be easy to fall into the pattern of looping repeatedly and trying to perfect every detail. But there is no reason to waste your good ideas. Why not turn them into finished songs?

When you develop a framework for how a finished song is constructed it becomes more easy to create finished songs from your loop ideas. In order to achieve this we need to understand the construction of an EDM song. EDM uses song structures that are quite different from the song structure of pop music. This is due to EDM not using vocals as much.

The arrangement of your EDM song is going to have a huge influence on how successful it will be. The end goal of most EDM music is to be played by DJ's and in that regard it needs to fulfill some requirements. As a listener of EDM you will notice some common themes. Most have an intro, build up, drop, break down and then repeat again. This isn't a coincidence, rather it is on purpose to allow DJs to easily mix in and out of the songs. To help you structure your songs it's a good idea to choose a reference track which you will study the structure of.

EDM is constructed to keep the energy going through highs and lows. The result is like a rollercoaster, building up energy, dropping it down and then repeating it again. However you don't have to follow the formulas. Breaking rules can produce profound results and happy accidents, so be creative as you wish.

Most EDM songs consist of four main structural parts:

- Intro
- Breakdown
- Build up
- Drop

Understanding how the construction of these four parts will help you to build a song. EDM songs will usually build up to a single powerful drop that is the focus of the song. Elements are usually added every four to eight bars and this is how you achieve the buildup effect. With this knowledge you can decide where to place your loop into the overall song structure. For example if your loop is from the drop then you can start to make an intro or build up to it. Now depending on the subgenres of EDM that you work in these four elements may differ. For example, Dubstep usually has quicker build ups than House.

Analyze other EDM songs to help you understand how a song is constructed. You can even copy out their structure so that you create a basic blueprint and know where your loop should be. Then finishing your song is simply a case of building up the other parts which you can change as you please.

Aim for a consistent vibe so all the different pieces work together which can be achieved by using some of the same parts for the whole song. Such as using the drop bassline for part of your build up or using parts of the melody in the intro and so on.

So how do you turn your loop into a song? The best way is to start with the drop. In most cases you start with your best ideas and those will likely make a great drop. When you know which part the song you're working with it will help you flesh out the whole song.

Once you know the section of the song you are working on and have a hot loop going you can split it into two by creating an alternative version of the first drop. This will help keep listeners hooked in and keep things fresh. With the drop done you can move to constructing the other parts of the song.

Intro

The intro of a song otherwise known as the beginning. It's standard practice for the intro to feature a stripped down making it easier for DJ's to mix in with. Sixteen bar intros or around thirty seconds have become more common in EDM as the listeners expect you to get straight to the point. Long intros can be saved for more underground genres.

Usually you can start out with some drums here. Not the full set but maybe the kick and a few hi hats. The drums used in your drop can be made more minimal and stripped down for the intro. Most tracks will also use some FX here as well such as a downfilter or some background ambience and tonal FX. sometimes you could use the lead sounds teasing the melody but not fully out there.

Tease things here and there but don't start off too strong, save that for the drop. The perfect intro will contain a balance of teasing and power. Teasing also aids in introducing the elements of your track to new listeners. For now it's all about progressing to the breakdown which you can sweep into with sweep FX and fills.

Breakdown

The intro is followed by a breakdown. Here the drums will usually stop to create a sense of anticipation for the listener. Breakdowns are often atmospheric and progressively build into the main hook of the song. You can also experiment with a big hit or impact coming in at the start of the breakdown. This gives an explosive and dramatic feeling that really adds energy to the track.

Buildup

When coming out of the break experiment with a small silence right before bringing in the main hook of the song in. This will create a big impact when the main part comes in. Coming out of the breakdown you really want to start to build things up to the drop. Use snares and instrumental elements to build things up. Add in some pitched risers that go up the scale. These can get gradually louder and faster to a climax.

Another common popular technique is to use a drop part, such as the lead or a bass line, and place it into the build up. Which makes for a much smoother transition and prepares the listener. Add in some reverse sounds and fills at the end of the buildup and a crash impact into the drop.

You will need lots of fades and automation to make everything nice and smooth. In addition you could even add a high-pass filter effect or other effects to your master channel to intensify it as you progress in the build up. This will not only help to transition from the breakdown to the drop, but also make the drop hit much harder. Ramp up the energy.

Drop
The last element, the drop, is the most important. It is the main hook of the song and the section where your productions have to really shine. Make sure this is the energetic high point and most memorable part of your song. If your song is all about melody, make sure you use the best melody here. This should be the full arsenal and will play for sixteen or thirty two bars with a some fills in the middle and a slightly different variation for the second half. In a lot of EDM genres the drop will then go into another breakdown, build up and then drop again. You can easily copy and paste those to the second part of your track. It's up you if you choose to introduce a new melody or chord progression later on.

Outro
For the end of your song you can do many different things. The most common thing to do is to gradually fade out. This could be the whole volume going down or taking things out one by one over sixteen bars. For example, take out the lead, the bass, the drums and so on. The volume fade is easier to do but the take out method usually sounds better. Just remember that music production is an art form. There is no ruleset for every song. Have an open mind and experiment with different things.

REMAKE: THE BEST WAY TO IMPROVE

The two essential components to becoming a better producer are time and effort. A great use of time and effort is to remake other music. Of course you can keep making originals but that won't expose you to new ideas and techniques as much as remaking will do. In addition you will rarely be at your full capabilities. For example if you learn piano and try to learn a specific song then you will notice when you make a mistake. When you work on original songs there is rarely a plan for how things will be put together. This will usually lead to going with what you know best and falling into habitual patterns. In that regard your not practicing with intent.

Remaking is no secret, it's been around for years. Beethoven studied Bach, authors study each other and of course nothing is made in a vacuum. You will learn so much from remaking other songs that can't be learned from books or YouTube videos. After practice and remake after remake making your own music will come much more naturally. In addition you will build up a wealth of ideas and knowledge. Then when producing new music, you will have an abundance of techniques and ideas to utilize. This will all lead to much more inspired EDM producing.

Now this has nothing to do with plagiarising or stealing. Because this is not about copying other music and passing it off as your own. Rather it is the process of remaking other songs purely for the purpose of practice and learning. When you set the goal to remake something it gives you a clear direction and forces you to figure out what works and what you need to accomplish. You will need to figure out how to create sounds, construct melodies, structure and every single component required to make an EDM song.

Remaking songs is almost like having a mentorship. Although it might be indirect, it's unlikely that you can call up an EDM superstar and ask them how they made a particular song. However you can remake their music and get inside of their mindset. Not only that but you will be exposed to their techniques and styles. In turn you might discover that they use a particular key or utilize build ups in a certain way and so on.

There really isn't a method for remaking songs. But there are some things you should consider. First of all, choose decent songs. Remakes can be time consuming so remaking something that's average than it will be time wasted. Ideally, you should only remake quality music in the genre you like. In addition try out other genres to learn more. However consider your skill level and don't attempt to remake more complicated songs. Build up your skill set first. If you are a beginner producer it's better to remake more simple EDM.

You don't need to get it exactly the same. There is no value in attempting to get it exactly the same. Always be focused on the value gained from the time spent. Purposeful remaking is beneficial even if you're just remaking basslines, intros and so on. To gain the most value remake the whole song and you will learn all the parts. Make it easy and find where instruments are in solo during the song. When remaking drums, listen at the start where they are most likely played alone. If your remaking a lead, check to see if it's alone somewhere.

Whist your working on remakes keep working on your originals. Ideally set aside some time to do remakes and some time for originals. With some well spent time of this you will have many projects which are essentially full tracks. By changing things around a little you can even turn them into your own songs. You will then notice yourself improving and developing critical listening skills.

HOW TO REMIX

Remixing is an integral part of EDM culture and as a producer it's a great way to open your mind to new ideas. The sooner you learn this skill, the better. As with remakes those skills and techniques that you learn from remixing can then be used for your originals.

Remixing helps you think creatively because it pushes you to try things you probably wouldn't try if you were working on originals. Add to that remixing brings awareness to your brand. There are many famous DJs who started out making mashups, bootlegs and remixes. It will certainly bring more attention to you.

Working with remixes is much easier than producing original songs. From the outset you will be provided with the melodies, sounds and ideas. This is great if your stuck in a creative rut. Starting with nothing can be daunting and remixing circumvents that fear.

To remix, you will need some source material. Decide on what result you're actually looking for before you start any remix. You can get involved in remix competitions where you will be provided with high quality music elements. This will give you inside knowledge of how the music is constructed and made. When your choosing which remix competitions to work on don't be put off if they don't offer much source material. Incidentally you don't need all the parts to remix a song, something as simple as vocal could be all that you need.

When you enter any remix competition it's important to note that your chances of winning are competitive and even if your work is good you might not get chosen as the winner. If you don't win then you can't releases it without their permission. Nevertheless working to deadlines and with official stems is a good thing to be involved with.

Finding remix competitions
Follow your favorite record labels or channels. Sometimes they run remix competitions independently. Also follow your favourite artists. Others might be hosted on a website such as Beatport Play. This is one of the most famous platforms and usually features tracks by big artists. Just sign up and you can get started.

Remix Comps (www.remixcomps.con) is another site for finding remix competitions. Additionally you can perform a search on Soundcloud for "remix contests" or "remix competitions". Then activate Google Alerts for "remix contest(s)" or "remix competition(s).

Pitching
If your really into a particular artists song then you can pitch to them or their label to remix it. In that regard you would normally benefit from having established yourself as a producer already. But don't shy away from it, believe in yourself. You could create a great remix and then pitch it. If you really believe in your remix then go ahead.

The best way you can approach them is through YouTube or Soundcloud. If they are huge artists that might be a little bit more difficult to get a reply. First, find their contact details and then send them your remix. If your lucky they might even send you the stems so you can improve on your ideas. Later on when your more famous, labels and artists may very well contact you for remixes. Make sure your branding and profile is strong to improve your chances of this happening.

Besides contacting people and remix competitions you can search Soundcloud for the keyword "stems." This will reveal any songs that have been made available to remix. However if you use them always contact the owner to ask if you can remix them. Alternatively you can sample songs, just remember that you will likely be infringing on the copyright and you would not be able to release it without permission.

Ideas
When your listening to potential songs to remix, you should get an idea of what they feature. Scan through the whole song for ideas. If you produce a particular EDM genre then it's beneficial to work with your strengths and find opportunities in that style. Remixing benefits from various genres but if your style is unique, then some remix styles won't be ideal. For example if your style is hard hitting beats then remixing a melodic trance song would not be a great fit.

Remixing is much easier then starting out with an original song. With a remix you will already have some source material. Maybe some stems, vocals and midi. You will also have some guidelines such as the genre, BPM and key. However those are not set in stone and its upto you to be as creative with your version of the remix as you wish.

If you have a vocal you can try out some new chords, melodies and things with it. Remixes can be as simple as changing some drums or as advanced as you wish. You could even change genres. As mentioned before if your known for a signature sound then this is a great idea. For example what works great with EDM remixes is turning pop songs into dancefloor hits. That could be something as simple as turning the chorus into a drop and making an extended intro. For example, Tiesto's Grammy award winning remix of John Legend's hit song "All of me". For this Tiesto simply added a kick drum beat to turn the song into something dancefloor friendly. Listen to other remixes for inspiration and to hear how they approached things.

Try stripping the song down to its fundamentals. You don't have to use all the parts. Simply build on the basic ideas. Typically when remixing you go with the key elements of the song such as the vocal or lead melody. This is what defines the track and you want to retain some of that so that people can identify with it. Try taking a minor melody and turning it into something major or take a few notes out of it. Experiment and test your ideas.

Changing Things
If you want to change the tempo of stems or acapellas you can utilize the warping function available in most DAW's. This allows you to go from one tempo up or down in BPM as you wish. Try to retain the quality as you do it. Plus or minus ten BPM is usually fine, anything more and you start to lose audio fidelity. In addition, make sure it's also kept in time. You can play a metronome or click to make sure everything is in it's correct place. If there are timing issues you can cut things and move them around. Most DAW warping functions will offer this tool as part of the warping.

Also with vocals you can do some really cool chop and pitch style effects. DJ Snake does this a lot and in fact it's really easy to do. FL Studio offers the Edison pitch tool to cut up samples and pitch them. Other DAW's you can use the audio editing tools to cut up and rearrange vocals. Or you can cut certain phrases of the vocal and load them into a sampler to play a new melody.

Content

You can also find the MIDI files for most songs through a simple Google search. In addition this method will also help you find acapellas. This will help you with unofficial remixes when your looking for the melodies or vocals of a song. You can then create your own versions of those. If you want acapellas for a typical song you can do one of two things.

- Search for the acapella online
- Create your own

Besides a Google search you can check out [Acapellas4U](#) which is one of the best websites for acapellas. [Beatport](#) also has a DJ Tools section with stems and acapellas.

Try the phase inversion technique to retrieve vocals from songs. You will need the instrumental of a song and then you can use the phase inversion technique. Essentially you play the instrumental with the original but with the phase inverted to cancel out all instruments and leave you with just the vocal. This isn't that effective though. Try as you wish and see how it sounds.

Legal

Remember that if you remix a song and distribute it online without permission, it's a bootleg. If you upload them to YouTube or Soundcloud without permission expect them to be taken down and your account could get banned. But don't let that put you off, you can still use it in your DJ sets. Just don't try to sell it.

If you really want to work around that legally you can produce a cover. Then you have taken the composition aways from the original without directly sampling it. In that regard you would need to re-record the vocal. However this can be a grey area of law. Seek legal advice before you distribute anything.

MIXING EDM

EDM demands huge synth lines, massive drums and beastly bass. With your song written it's time to start making it sound big. Mixing is the first step.

Prepare
Before you start mixing you need to get in the right mind set. Be well rested and inspired. It's a good idea to take a break from you song for at least a week before you start to mix it. Try mixing in the morning to ensure your energy is highest and your ears are fresh. Remove all distractions such as internet connections on your production computer and have your phone away from you. Also make sure you have sufficient time planned ahead for mixing. Between six to ten hours should be plenty of time and that should include some regular short breaks.

Start with good sounds
The mixing process really starts the moment you begin producing. From the outset you need to be selecting sounds that are of the best quality. This will make the mixdown much better and easier. Choose samples and sounds that hit the right frequencies and work well together. Remember, what matters most is how good it all sounds together and not in solo. A hot lead might sound good in solo but could make your drums dull. Spend the time and perfect your sounds before you start mixing down. You can also switch out some sounds during the mixing stages. This is often a better solution to trying to fix them with mixing.

Stems

Use stems when mixing. This involves bouncing all of your channels down to audio files and then importing them to a new project. Mentally this commits you to how things sound, frees up processing power and makes you more efficient. Organize your projects and it will save you a lot of time. You can group certain sounds together such as all the drums or all the FX and so on. This will also save your CPU power by doing things on one channel instead of multiple repetitions.

Reference
Choose some reference tracks that are mixed well and are a great end result to aim for. These work the best if they are in the same key as your song since instruments sound different in other keys.

Clean
Maybe at this stage you might want to add some things or even take out anything unnecessary. Be critical of what you add, everything needs its purpose and place. The more you add to your track the more frequencies will build up. Be aware that you will need to leave lots of space below 200 HZ for your kick, bass and sub. Use EQ to clean up any sharp resonant frequencies. Nothing should stick out too much. You can sweep a parametric EQ with a narrow Q band to hear those and then attenuate them.

Mono
EDM is destined for the club and most club sound systems are in mono. Therefore your song needs to be mono compatible. Be critical of too much stereo imaging on your sounds. Keep testing your mix in mono by using a mono tool on the master channel. You can still use wideners and so on, just make sure you check if any sounds disappear when doing that.

Vocals and bass tend to work best at the center and are often in mono. You can still create width to them and an easy way to do that is with panning. Pan one sound left and another right. Then detune one up a few cents (increment of a half tone) and the other down a few cents. This will give the impression that its a double take or a stereo recording.

Keep anything under 200 Hz mono. This will avoid phase cancellation and again club sound systems have the bass in mono. In addition bass is omni-directional, which means you can't determine where it's coming from anyway. If you want your bass to sound wide, add a mid bass layer with stereo effects. Again, check in mono to identify any phase cancellation.

Listen in context
When your mixing avoid using the solo button on channels. You need to hear things in context of the mix because they will sound different together. Sometimes you might need to switch the sound to another preset or sample. That can often be a better solution then applying lots of mixing processing.

Hierarchy
When you approach your mix decide on which is the most important element of the mix and then mix around that. From the start you should have an idea of which elements will be needed, what their frequency content is and which are the most important. Experiment with their order to achieve the results you want. Usually it would be something like as follows.

1. Vocals
2. Synth lead
3. Kick

4. Bass
5. Snare

Do a rough guidance mix
This is one of the most important steps to get your track to sound better. The best point to start mixing at is the drop or the most important section of the song. This guarantees that things will hit the hardest here and you can then mix around that.

Set the master fader at 0dB and pull all the channels in your song down to muted. Select the most important channel in the song, usually that will be the kick or vocal in EDM. Have that peak around -6dB. By staying at lower levels it will give you space to bring all the other channels into the mix. Mix them in one by one and follow that sequence by importance. The master channel should not be peaking above -6dB which will help for for mastering later on.

Make sure when you bring sounds in that they don't compromise the most important elements as you add them to the mix. Do they sound good together? If no, change things up. Try out different kick or drum samples, presets and so on. Everything should be tested in the context of the mix.

Group and bus
Make use of grouping and bussing. You can group similar sounds together and process them as one. For example all the drum hits can go to one channel. Or all the vocals to one channel. Then you can apply processing to them as a whole and make it cohesive.

Sidechain Compression

Sidechain compression is an elite trick of the EDM trade. We can use it to clean up a mix and make things stand out. In essence sidechain compression will turn down one sound so that another sound can be heard clearly. The most common use is to sidechain the bass and kick so that the bass ducks every time the kick hits.

Xfer LFO tool is a great plugin for sidechaining. Just apply it to the bass channel with a ¼ rhythm. You can then adjust the envelope for how it ducks. Alternatively if your song is not on a 4/4 beat you can use sidechaining on a send and return to duck parts. Just apply a compressor with the sidechain function to the channel you want to duck. Then choose the input source as the channel you want to be the sound that ducks it. You can then adjust the envelope for the ducking.

EQ
EQ allow us to reduce or boost the gain of specific frequency bands. There are four different EQ shapes commonly used:

- High Pass: Used to remove low-end frequencies.
- Low Pass: Used to remove high-end frequencies.
- Bell: Used to boost or cut at a given range.
- Shelf: Reduce or boost high end or low end.

When using EQ it's better to cut than boost. This reduces the build up of frequencies that can make your mix clip. For example to make a sound brighter, try reducing the bass and mid frequencies. Then increase the channel volume. You should high pass filter the majority of your sounds to give more room in the mix. Many record sounds have unwanted low frequencies. Even sounds such as hi hats. Apply a simple hi pass filter to clean them up.

When you want to boost with EQ have a purpose for doing it. Such a helping something cut through a mix. All EQ decisions should for a purposes not because you got told to by some guide. Listen, test, and then decide.

There are certain frequency ranges that produce characteristic sounds:

- Sub frequencies: Below 100Hz
- Heavy/ Muddy: 180-225 Hz
- Nasal/ Boxy: 400-600 Hz
- Ears Most Sensitive: 1.6-3 kHz
- Airy/Bright: 10 kHz and up

Compression
Compression and EQ are the fundamental tools used to help sculpt a mix. EQ can be used to remove unnecessary frequencies first. After fixing those problems the compressor can even out volume differences and give an overall louder sound. This make it easier to hear in the mix. Essentially it will take the quiet parts of a sound and boost them to be closer to the louder parts. This is a popular effect in EDM but use it sparingly to avoid squashing your sounds too much.

Compressors have the following common functions.

- Attack: When the compressor is activated. If sounds have too much transients you can reduce them with a fast attack. Alternatively you can boost them by letting them through and then compressing the rest of the sound. Some compressors have an automatic attack which will follow a compression algorithm.
- Release: When the compressor lets go of the sound. Sometimes you might want to compress the whole

sound. Sometimes you might want to compress a smaller part. Release can be used to set that. Some compressors have an automatic release which will follow a compression algorithm.
- Threshold: This is for setting the amplitude of when compressor starts to compress. Setting it at the top will catch the very loudest sounds. Pushing it more will squash the sound.
- Ratio: This is the intensity of compression. Higher ratios push the compression more.
- Gain: after compression you will want to bring the reduction in amplitude back up. Gain does that. Some compressors have an automatic gain which will follow a compression algorithm.

Reverb

Todays sound in EDM is pretty dry. However there is still a lot of reverb in use and it is great for adding life and width to your sounds. It works best when applied to a bus send. Set up a new group channel with a reverb on then send your sounds to that. Make sure it is set to wet %100.

Reverbs in EDM are usually heavily ducked with the source sound which will give you a dry source with a nice reverb tail. You can achieve this by sidechaining the reverb with your source. Here are some basic guidelines to using reverb:

- Drums: Try a room-reverb with high damping to make them sound more real.
- Bass: A simple reverb similar to the drums will add life whilst not taking up too much space.
- Vocals: Hall reverb works well. Use sparingly and be careful to check mono compatibility and also that any high frequencies are not washed out.

- Synths: Big reverbs work well. Try sidechaining them to keep the lead clean with some nice reverb tail.
- Pads: Usually benefit from big and lush reverb.

Volume automation

Utilize volume automation to make changes across the whole song. Some sections of your song might require different levels for instruments. For example maybe the drop lead needs to be louder than in the build up. Or the vocals work well quieter in the breakdown. You can use volume automation to turn up or turn down those parts as you wish. Incidentally you can automate pretty much any parameter in most DAWs. Maybe you want to send more reverb or high pass certain sections. Be creative.

Use a Spectrum Analyser

Spectrum analysers will show you a visual representation of your songs frequency content, amplitude and stereo information. This is essential for checking your mix against your reference. However don't rely too much on it, trust your ears first.

Test

Before you move to the mastering phase listen to your mix on all your headphones, speaker setups, cars, and sound systems. Take a break for a few days and come back with fresh ears. Don't mix for more than a couple of hours each time. Otherwise you start to lose objectivity. Take a break, get some air and get back to it later on.

Ask your friends, family and peers for feedback. Fresh ears will give you a new perspective. But don't ask them if they life it because most will say yes to avoid hurting your feelings. Instead ask them for critical feedback. This is vital for your development. You can also make use of websites such as www.synthshare.com for feedback.

Test the mix down at different levels. For the majority of the time mix at quieter levels to minimize ear fatigue. Now and then turn the levels up and see how it sounds. Human hearing is sensitive to different frequencies depending on their amplitude. Therefore checking your mixes at different levels overall will help you achieve a better mix.

MASTERING

Well mastered EDM is critical to getting DJs to play your songs. The process is often misunderstood and perceived as someone simply cranking a mix through a limiter and adding some shine with fancy gear. Sometimes you may well send your song to be mastered. However it's a good idea to get familiar with the process.

The goal of mastering is to turn a mixed song into a finished a product ready for distribution. Whether that be for streaming, broadcasting, DJ's or downloads. Mastering concerns the final stereo mixdown of a song after it has been mixed.

Good mastering requires an acoustically accurate environment as well as transparent monitoring. Invest in a subwoofer for your studio so you can hear lower frequencies. Alternatively you can use a SUBPAC which is a wearable bass system allowing you to feel the lowest frequencies. In addition make use analyzers so that you can see the lowest frequencies.

The first step is to listen through the song with fresh ears. Listen for any technical mishaps or things that stick out. Usually the common flaws are, excessive bass or excessive sharp high-end frequencies. Often producers also push their mixes too high and clipping or phase issues occur. Mastering can't fix a bad mix. In extreme cases it's best to go back to the drawing board and mix again.

After forming an idea of what you need to do to the track you can start to address things. Try not to go overboard otherwise you will sacrifice the character of the mix. Remember that these are guidelines and each song will have differences that require alternative approaches and techniques.

How to master EDM with iZotope Ozone
iZotope Ozone currently on its 8th edition is an entire suite of plugins for mastering. It's a great way for beginners to start mastering their own music.

Bass management
Start with bass management. Apply an EQ with a high-pass setting to filter out anything below 30 HZ. Go with the steepest slope.

Exciter
Next add an exciter to brighten things up. The exciter comes as a multiband exciter so you can split the frequency spectrum into four different bands and then boost or cut the harmonics in each band. The difference between an exciter and an EQ is that with an exciter you boost the harmonics. This can be done in many different modes including, warm, retro, tape, tube, triode and dual triode. These emulate analog devices to saturate those areas in a harmonically pleasing way. Experiment with each of the types and apply as required. Use the dry and wet mix to make it more subtle.

Compression
Next add some vintage compressor to control dynamics along with some buss compression. Set the gain reduction, you don't want too much. The two and a half to one ratio is fine. Set the attack time a bit slower to let the transients come through and keep things punchy. Again we are being very subtle. Apply the threshold slowly and hear the results. You can do this in multi band mode also to tame peaks in a

different band. Then add on auto gain to automatically adjust the gain to compensate for the loss of volume encountered in the compression process.

Saturation
Use the vintage tape add effect to add saturation or warmth. You can add this in the different frequency bands as you wish. Be subtle and retain the songs character without going overboard.

Stereo Imager
Use the imager to do a nice spread on the mix. You can spread each individual four different bands. EDM works well with a narrow low end and then spreading out to the high end. It can be tempting to push these wide but it just messes with your with your phase coherence. Make sure the mix is always mono compatible. There's also a built-in correlation meter which you want to more or less stay at zero or above to maintain proper phase coherency.

Maximizer
Use a Maximizer to get some extra gain at the end. This is a brick wall limiter. Just pull your threshold down to get some gain boosting. The limiting is quite transparent across the four available modes. However don't go overboard with it. Try to maintain a transient heavy song. The kick and drums need to come through.

Once the mastering is how you want it to be you can mix out the files for the medium they're to be released on. That could be WAV or Mp3 as required with meta-data embedded) or AIFF and so on. You can deliver a different master for downloads then you would from what you might play at a club. Test those out.

DIGITAL AUDIO WORK STATION (DAW)

The DAW is the central working unit for making EDM. Before we look at the options it's important to note that there is no best DAW. It all depends on how you work and what you like to use. The kind of music you make and the techniques you prefer will influence that.

Try before you buy.
Most DAW manufacturers offer a demo version for people to try. Testing with a demo will reveal whether you are going to like it or not. Consider factors such as the price, resources and workflow. The main factor to consider besides price should be workflow. This is the way you produce and arrange music. The DAW that allows you to do this seamlessly is the best option for you.

There are five major DAW's out there which are really great for EDM production. Each of these are easy to get started with and offer a wealth of guidance. Most come with a manual and online support at the least. Without further ado let's take a look at them.

Ableton Live
Ableton Live is currently the most popular DAW for EDM producers. It is easy to learn for anyone, with or without experience. It was designed for both live performance and music production. Comes with over 11 GB of samples, three instruments and over thirty effects. Simple, intuitive, design and workflow are central to it's design.

Used By: Jack U, Major Lazer, Hardwell, Maddix and More.

FL Studio
FL Studio is the underdog of EDM production. It offers an intuitive approach to making EDM. Popular among dub-step and trap music producers because it is easy to program beats with the sequencer. Comes with some great synths and tools for producers to utilize. Check out the vocal editing options in Edison.

Used By: Makj, Afrojack, Martin Garrix, Jay Hardway, DJ Snake and More.

Logic Pro X
Logic Pro X has been a choice of many EDM producers for a long time. It is stable, reliable and easy to work with. Included with it is a solid library of sounds and some great factory instruments. Logic is available for Mac computers only. Sorry Windows users.

Used By: Calvin Harris, Axwell Ingrosso, Jonas Blue, Swindali, David Guetta and More.

Steinberg Cubase
Steinberg Cubase was technically the first DAW ever made. Viewed largely as a pioneer of music software. Very stable even with large projects. Includes some great tools which make an awesome environment for creating EDM. Also some awesome in built instruments.

Used By: Knife Party, Junkie XL, Chase & Status, Infected Mushroom and more

Reason

Reason can be a bit intimidating at first glance because of its intricate interface. However it is easy to learn. The rack is full of awesome instruments and effects that are all of very high quality. You can mix and mash these together as you please and the processing required is minimal. The only drawback is that third party plug-ins aren't supported as of now.

Used By: Rick Rubin, The Prodigy, Claude Von Stroke and more

MUST HAVE PLUGINS

In EDM production it is easy to get lost in downloading more and more plug ins. However what is far better is to know a few tools really well. The plugins you need really depends on the music you are creating. A one size fits all solution doesn't exist. Incidentally the stock plug ins packaged with your DAW are pretty damn good these days.

As time goes on you will find certain plugins you prefer. That will also depend on the level of skill you are at. Sometimes you will outgrow and need something more advanced. But regardless of your skill level, price is still going to be a huge factor in what plugins you own. The important thing to note here is that an expensive plugin does not necessarily mean it is better or that it's going to make your music sound better.

Nothing beats talent and good sounds.

VIRTUAL STUDIO INSTRUMENTS

Virtual instruments are software versions of an instrument. That could be a real world instrument such as a piano. Or something completely unique for software. There are so many available for you to start making sounds with. Let's take a look at some of the most popular for EDM.

Arturia V Collection
This is a collection of ten virtual instruments that cover analogue style synthesis. If you want to create some fat leads and big bass then this is a great choice.

Kontakt
Every EDM producer needs a good sampler to load up sounds and play them across the scale. Kontakt is one of the best on the market. It also comes with some great sound banks which means you have access to orchestras and more at your fingertips.

Native Instruments FM8
This is a more advanced synth that is used by producers including Skrillex and Knife Party. Has some great presets and ability to create morphed sounds.

Native Instruments Komplete Ultimate
Komplete is a collection of instruments, effects and sounds. Included is a huge library of synths, samples and packs. You can create pretty much any sound with this. Drums, bass, real instruments and synthetic ones. Essential for your productions.

Nexus

Nexus is a ROMpler which means it plays back sample libraries from expansion packs. You can modify those sounds with the inbuilt, EQ, envelopes, filters and so on. The patches are super high quality and are a must have for EDM production.

NI Massive

This is the synth for dubstep. Amazing lfo and modulation section for creating those wobbly basslines. In addition can make so much more with its diverse wavetables and intuitive programming options.

Reaktor 6

If your looking to get advanced and create your own sounds from scratch then Reaktor 6 is the synth for you. Offers tons of flexibility from designing and wiring your own synths to creating unique custom sounds. For advanced users.

Spectrasonics Omnisphere

Omnisphere is a beast of a virtual studio instrument and is epic at making complex sounds and atmospherics. Used mostly by movie composers but can be great for EDM. With over fifty gigabytes of sample libraries it gives you access to incredible instruments. From classical sounds to the most bizarre sounds. Load up some presets and get inspired.

Spire

Spire is a great sounding additive hybrid synth that works really well for creating modern EDM leads. You can even create some complex sounds using the modulation matrix and lush filters.

Sylenth1

This is one of the go to synths for EDM. Has a warm sound and some great factory presets to get you going. Unlimited possibilities for creating everything from the complex to the big, simple sounds. Heard in countless EDM hits.

U-he Diva
Inspired by the classic analogue synthesizer, the Minimoog. Offers an analog-like sound quality and is easy to use. Great for creating big and full sounds.

X-FER Records Serum
Serum dethorned Massive as the king of wavetable synthesis. It is an amazing synthesizer that can create analog style patches and amazing sounds. You can even import your own wavetables to acquire more sound palettes. Great LFO, freedom to program, high quality effects and more.

PLUG INS

Plugins are there to plug into your channels and enhance, modulate or clean up your sounds. They can be used on both midi, instrument, group and audio channels. There are so many different kinds of plug ins and below are some of the most popular listed by category for EDM production.

Analyzers

Voxengo Span, Waves and Izotope
Every project needs a spectrum analyzer. This will help you to understand frequencies and their relationship to pitch. Waves and Izotope also offer some great analyzers.

Delay

Soundtoys EchoBoy
Models classic units and has various delay types.

Waves H-Delay
This is a great delay with an old school analog feel with a modern touch. Use it to give vocals the feeling of more space or add depth to your sounds.

Distortion

Fabfilter Saturn
The perfect blend of complex and simple saturation or distortion. The standard presets are easy to get you going and you can modulate them even more to create your own sounds.

Izotope Trash
A great option for distortion. Smash things to the next level. Used by Skrillex.

Camelphat
Has an amazing distortion section offering four different types.

Dynamics

AOM Invisible Limiter
EDM needs to be big and loud. But you still want it to sound good and not squashed or distorted. The AOM Invisible Limiter comes in with transparent limiting and it can be pushed so hard that your track won't distort.

Izoptope Ozone
Mixing and mastering suite of high quality plug ins. Easy to use and great results.

Oxford Inflator
Make your sounds louder and fuller.

SPL Transient Designer
Add this powerful tool to your plug in arsenal. This weapon can be used to add punch to your drums and plucked sounds.

Sonnox Dynamics
A multi-purpose processor with functions for gating, side-chain, compression, limiting, EQ and a warmth circuit. Dynamics control is an essential part of EDM production. This is a workhorse that gets the job done well.

Sonnox Inflator

Use this to make your sounds bigger. This increases the perceived volume of a sound without affecting dynamic range. The end result is a bigger version of the original signal.

UAD 1176 Classic Limiter Collection

This is a famous modelled compressor based on hardware. Works well on drums. In order to use this you will need a UAD system.

Waves CLA-2A

Waves are an industry leader for creating unrivaled plug-ins. The Waves CLA-A2 is a compression plugin emulated on tube compressors. These are simple to use and work amazing on Leads, Vocals, and Bass.

Xfer Records OTT Compressor

This one is actually a free tool. Use it to add color and gloss to your sounds.

Effects

Camelphat

Distortion, lfos, filters and effect. All can be routed as you wish. Smash things up and make them interesting.

SugarBytes Effectrix

Super cool effects plug in for manipulating your sounds across a grid. Twist your sounds beyond recognition to create something unique.

Filters

FabFilter Pro Q2

One of the best EQ plugins for mixing and mastering EDM. Allows you to enhance or treat frequency bands with clean transparency. The Linear Phase mode prevents any phase issues from occurring when cutting frequencies.

FabFilter Simplon
Filters are essential for EDM production. Fabfilter is one of the best filter plugins available. It offers great sound and harmonically pleasing resonance. Easy to use and affordable.

Misc

Waves One KNOB
A simple to use plug in that offers great quality, saturation, brightness, side chain and filtering.

Musical

Odesi
Music composition software to help you write melodies, chords and add mood to your music. In addition can detect the key and scale of audio.

Reverb

UVI Sparkverb
If you are looking for a clean sounding reverb that can create light ambiences to huge soundscapes all whilst being light on processing then this is your answer.

Stereo Imaging

Mid Side Tool
Control the mid and side of a signal with ease.

Flux Stereo Tool
Great for stereo imaging and panning. Give your sounds space. Waves An amazing stereo imager and panning tool. Waves and Izotope also offer great stereo imaging tools.

Waves S1
Easily spread or narrow your sounds.

Vocals

Melodyne
When your working with vocals there will always be some treatment required. Melodyne comes in to help here. Allows you to clean up the timing and tuning of vocals. Absolutely essential for recording vocals.

GET SIGNED

So you have your EDM song ready. Your happy with it and ready to share it with the world. Begin your journey to EDM superstardom!

The first step to take towards getting signed is to have great music. Finished products that you believe in. After that there are a few more things an EDM artist will need to do in order to get signed

Branding
These days you need more than good music to stand out. Just uploading your music isn't enough. Even if it is really amazing. Your chances of being noticed and then signed will increase greatly if you have professional press materials and strong branding. Take a good profile shot, have a decent logo and a concurrent theme to your profile. If your lost for ideas look at some of your idols and study what you like. Then try to incorporate some of these elements into your designs.

Leave the best possible first impression you can. When labels listen to your music, chances are they are going to analyze your online appearance. If it looks poor then your reputation is mirrored to them so that will influence them to sign your track or not. Keep it professional and music related only. Make an official website, have strong branding and always try to be unique.

Social media is also important to achieving a successful EDM career. You need at least Facebook, Instagram, Soundcloud and Twitter so that you can contact with DJ's, producers and labels. The majority of big EDM labels listen to music on Soundcloud. In most cases use this to upload your demos and then send to them. Make sure they are set to **private only** before you sign anything.

Contacting Labels

Having connections with labels is the best way to get signed. If your constantly networking with DJs and producers then they can help get you in touch with the labels. Always be growing your network, send your music out for feedback, attend shows and be social. When it comes to formally contacting a label you can send them an email of your demo.

Come up with a list of suitable labels. You can find out how they accept demos through Google. Just type: label naem + demo. Some might have their own page for submitting demos. Others will accept email and it should follow a simple format.

Subject line: artist name - track name.
Then open the email with:
hello, I would like to share with you my latest song for consideration.
Artist name - Track name
Private Soundcloud link
Thank you

Name
Twitter account
Instagram account
Facebook account
Website

Keep it simple and straight to the point. Be patient and wait for them to reply. Don't send any follow up emails. If they are interested then they will get back to you. Keep the emails private. If you send emails to multiple labels put them in the BCC section so that no one knows about others being contacted. Labels want to feel special and that it is only you contacting them. Replies can take up to a month or more so don't sit around waiting, move on with your producing. If you have more songs to send wait at least another month. You want to avoid bombarding them. Keep an eye on your Soundcloud stats to see who is playing your tracks.

Tips
Only send your absolute best work and never send unfinished, unmastered songs or demos.

Avoid using copyrighted material
Clearing it requires a lot of effort and money. Labels aren't keen on that. I know there is stuff out there that is copyrighted but it is either coming from big labels who cleared it or from smaller ones who fly under the radar.

Don't send remixes or bootlegs
These are difficult to be signed officially. Anything like those save for your own channels and packs.

Send quality over quantity
Only send in your very best tracks and do it every other month or so. Force yourself to filter for the best.

CONCLUSION

There you have it, everything you need to produce EDM! The next thing you need to do is fire up your DAW and use what you have learned. Turn it into a hit EDM song.

Produce it
Apply the techniques from this book then use the mixing and mastering guide to make it sound huge.

Take it out and test it.
Play it to your friends, family and if you spin a club try it out there. How do people react to it? Should you change anything? When your happy you can send it out to some labels. Rinse and repeat.

Become better
Over time you will become a better EDM producer. If you stick with it and keep trying new things then that's a guarantee. Challenge yourself to try new things and learn more.

Mentors
Make sure you have good mentors around you to give you feedback and help you realize your vision. Be a part of the community both online and in the real world.

Feedback
Have an open mind to feedback and never take it personally. View it as constructive criticism to improve.

I wish you all the best and look forward to hearing your music on the mainstage and festivals soon.

Catch up with me at

www.tommyswindali.com

www.swindali.com

Thanks for Reading!

What did you think of, **Electronic Dance Music Production: The Advanced Guide On How to Produce Music for EDM Producers**

I know you could have picked any number of books to read, but you picked this book and for that I am extremely grateful.

I hope that it added at value and quality to your everyday life. If so, it would be really nice if you could share this book with your friends and family by posting to Facebook and Twitter.

If you enjoyed this book and found some benefit in reading this, I'd like to hear from you and hope that you could take some time to post a review. Your feedback and support will help this author to greatly improve his writing craft for future projects and make this book even better.

I want you, the reader, to know that your review is very important and so, if you'd like to leave a review, all you have to do is click here and away you go. I wish you all the best in your future success!

Keep upto date with me:

www.tommyswindali.com
www.swindali.com

Thank you and good luck!

Tommy Swindali

BONUS: GHOST PRODUCING

Ghost producing is an agreement between a music producer composing a track for another artist who then releases that track under their own name. The ghost producer will normally be paid a flat fee upfront for their work.

For a lot of established EDM DJs they use ghost producers to help realize their visions. That could mean them sitting down with the ghost producer and directing them or just selecting on of their songs which they like. Nowadays there is a lot that goes into being an EDM artist and you will find behind every EDM superstar there are teams of people.

Many producers go with ghost producing because they prefer to stay out of the limelight. Maybe you love producing but want to keep your life private. Well that's a great idea for you to ghost produce for others. That way you can fulfill your passion and still get to see people enjoy your music. The fame isn't for everyone and there is a lot of pressure with it.

Once the big names start supporting your music it's going to open a lot of doors. In fact it's well known that Martin Garrix started out ghost producing and then got introduced to label bosses through that. Who you know is so important these days.

So many big EDM hits were ghost produced. It's the role of the ghost producer to make the vision of the client into a reality. The amount of money you can make depends on a number of factors. That can start as little as $300 and go right over $20,000. It all depends on the calibre of artists you work with and of course your credentials.

If your looking to get started www.edmghostproducer.com is a website where any producer can upload their tracks for sale. They do have an approval process and not every song is listed, but if you have good music try.

BONUS: 18 THINGS EVERY EDM PRODUCER NEEDS TO SUCCEED

One
You will need a computer or a laptop. A laptop is much easier because you can produce on anywhere, anytime. Mac is usually better long term but if you know about specs go with Windows.

Two
You will need a digital audio workstation (DAW). This is at the centre of your computer music production studio. Use it to hold your projects and work on them.

Three
You will need a set of monitor speakers to playback your music. Make sure you set them up correctly in your room. For best results acoustically treat your room.

Four
You will need a pair of monitor headphones. Nowadays the majority of music is played back on smaller speakers such as headphones. If it doesn't sound good on headphones people are probably not going to like it much.

Five
You will need a MIDI keyboard to play in melodies and chords. Invest in some music training and take your EDM to the next level.

Six

Back support, take care of your back and use a pillow or a comfortable chair for those long hours of producing. Live long and strong!

Seven
Obsession. Eat sleep and breathe EDM production. It takes at least ten thousand hours to be professional in something.

Eight
Music theory, learn scales and keys. This is the fundamental of good music. You don't need to be a Mozart but a little helps massively.

Nine
Find a mentor. They will help you to progress and become better much more quickly then on your own. If you can work with someone face to face its best but online is great too.

Ten
You will need, samples. You need samples to construct your song. Sign up for a Splice account. Use the best ones available.

Eleven
You will need, Plug ins and Virtual Instruments to create and control your sounds. Take a look at the chapter in this book about the best plugins.

Twelve
You will need mixing skills to turn your project into a big mix. Practice makes perfect, keep going and push through the challenges.

Thirteen

You will need, mastering to create a high quality finished song. Take ownership of your songs and do it yourself.

Fourteen
You will need a logo so that people can remember who you are and start branding yourself online. Try www.fiverr.com for some affordable designers.

Fifteen
You will need need to join EDM networks to keep upto to date and network. Get on the best forums and engage with members.

Sixteen
You will need to build your social network presence. This will help you get signed. Facebook, Instagram, Soundcloud are all essential. Be active.

Seventeen
Build fans and friends to support your music. Have a good attitude and add value to people. Reach out to new people.

Eighteen
You will need need good music. This is the most important factor for you to grow and succeed as an EDM artist. You can do it!

In The Mix: Discover The Secrets to Becoming a Successful DJ

Contents

Introduction

Beginner's Guide To DJ Equipment Setups
    DJ Controller
        Newmark NVII
        Reloop Terminal Mix Eight Reloop
        Kontrol S4 MK2
        Pioneer DDJ SB

Professional's Guide To DJ Equipment Setups
    CDJ
    DJM900 Nexus
    Laptop DJ
    USB

Where Do DJs Get Their Music?
    How to Understand Genres

How To Organize And Manage Your Music
    Rekordbox
    Mixed In Key
    Serato
    Traktor

How to Mix Like a Pro
    Theory
    Standard Mixing
    Bass Cut
    Mixing With Sound Color FX
    Mixing With Beat FX
    Filter In and Out
    Vinyl Stop/Drop In

Backspin
Loop

Mashing Things Up

How to Get Gigs
Management
Booking Agents

Branding & Marketing
Producing
Electronic Press Kit (EPK)

Everything You Need to Know Before You Play Your First Gig
Tip One
Tip Two
Tip Three
Tip Four
Tip Five
How to Read a Crowd
Working with an MC
Dealing With Nerves

FAQ and Top Tips

About The Author

Introduction

A lot of people have the misconception that DJing is really hard to get into but it's actually really simple. All you need is the passion and you can start out with something as simple as a smartphone, or a DJ controller. anybody can be a DJ as long as they work hard and are motivated to achieve their goals

In essence, DJing is taking music that already exists and changing it in a way that is pleasing for a crowd. What's great about it is that you can combine different genres and songs into one idea. DJing creates this, sort of, combined culture that really unites many fans. There is so much you can do as a DJ from mixing in the bedroom to stirring up a storm on the main stage.

Nowadays, there are so many different ways to DJ. What could originally only be done on turntables, by early pioneers such as Grandmaster Flash and Carl Cox, can now be done with many more pieces of equipment. There are many amazing programs now, such as Traktor Pro, Serato and Rekordbox and even applications for tablets and touchscreens. If you prefer the old school ways you can still use turntables or even CDJs, controllers and extra hardware. There are so many different combinations. All of these really do the same thing, and that's to mix songs.

When your staring out, take the time to study DJs and find the music that inspires you. Whether it's listening to podcasts, watching live sets, or just really looking them up online. Observe and take in what it means to be a great DJ. Hone your skills with regular practice and you will soon be able to play at any club.

Festivals and club culture have created massive DJ stars and turned it into a popular past time. The current climate for is highly competitive and you will need a strategy to stand out. Because besides DJing, there are many more tasks to do. For example DJs need to promote themselves, network and maybe eventually produce music to get more gigs. Whether you are a beginner or more. experienced the contents of this book will help you.

Beginner's Guide To DJ Equipment Setups

The absolute easiest way to get started DJing is with your smartphone. There are an absolute slew of DJing apps and my favorite is Algorithms DJ. It's pretty much a fully fledged DJing solution in your pocket and is really easy to use. It features a full mixer with some effects that aren't even available on hardware and there are individual deck controls. With its Spotify integration you don't need to download music on your phone. Actually you can just download it off the cloud. If you want something more hands on then the next level is the DJ controller.

DJ Controller

If you're thinking about a DJ system for home it doesn't really make sense to have the nightclub equivalent. Unless you're making an awful lot of money from your DJing or money's no object. DJ controllers offer an affordable solution. Essentially the controller is two to four CDJ's combined with a mixer in one piece of equipment. In most you can also input microphones, headphones and output to speakers.

The controller is going to connect to your laptop or your tablet and will also be running a DJ software. You can link these up with Traktor or Serato software which will hold your library of music and allow playback on virtual decks that you control with controller. Let's take a look at the five best DJ controllers.

Newmark NVII

A dual CDJ, four channel controller. This allows you to have up to four decks playing simultaneously. Aside from looking great and offering full color screens the NBI offers an ultra fast response of operation and seamlessly beat matching to make it a strong choice.

Reloop Terminal Mix Eight Reloop

A four deck performance controller, great for mixing lots of songs. The controller was developed to work specifically with Serato DJ software and it responds well to the requirements of professional club DJ's. Offers creative effects manipulation and unique mixing possibilities.

Kontrol S4 MK2

A dual CDJ, four channel controller allowing up to four decks playing simultaneously. A great choice for DJ's who want professional features, ease of use and portability. Combines a high quality mixer with professional grade, built in sound card and an intuitive interface that works with Traktor Pro 2 software.

Pioneer DDJ SB

The best two channel option on the market. Responsive performance pads and large jog wheels make it easy to mix and mash up live music. Offers low latency jog wheels for great scratch response and accuracy. High-pass filters combined on the cross fader offer both volume and base filters with just one hand. Great for smooth mixes.

Professional's Guide To DJ Equipment Setups

The industry standard for DJ's in a nightclub is currently two to four, CDJ's and a DJ mixer which will go out to the main soundsystem. The DJ will have their own monitor feed to listen to and of course headphones to listen to the song that is not playing. Pioneer currently dominate the professional DJ equipment market. Denon are making a strong efforts but Pioneer remain king.

CDJ

The Pioneer CDJ 2000 Nexus and Nexus 2 are currently the club standard for CDJ's and will likely stay that way for the next five years.

Let's take a look at the CDJ Nexus 2. On the left side, there is a flashing USB input which shows you if the CDJ is currently in use. Upto four CDJ's can be linked together and played off of one USB. This makes it easy for the next DJ coming in to use their USB without disturbing you.

To start, first the USB stick goes in and you select a source. Select link if the USB is in the adjacent CDJ. You can select the source you are using on the buttons to the left. Which are Rekordbox, link, USB, sd, disc. Sd slot is below the USB and disc is at the bottom of the unit. Once loaded you can browse through the folders by turning the dial to the appropriate folder. When you find the song you want to play, simply press down and it is loaded to go. You can organize music to your preferences with Rekordbox software before you use your USB and then export the settings. When you finish playing there is a USB stop switch. Make sure you hold this down and wait for it to be OK to remove.

Below the USB input is a bank of hot cues. Hot cues are great if you want to seamlessly skip forward or backwards without stopping the play. They are color-coded as well backlit. There are upto eight hot cues available in two banks. Bank two can be be found by clicking the bank buttons at the bottom. You can add and delete hot cues on the player using the controls there or alternatively before you mix using Rekordbox software.

Below the hot cues is a paddle switch to move the play direction forwards, reverse or slip rev, which is cool for quick cuts. At the bottom left you have track search and search buttons for skipping or searching through tracks. Then you have the cue and play/pause buttons. The cue button will always default to where it was last set. When you pressed it will stop there. On the right is the cue loop to shift the memory cues which are associated with the cue button. Add memory or delete is for making or deleting memory cues.

The large digital panel screen allows you to browse through playlists, select songs and organize them by your preferences. This could be by bpm, alphabet or key for example. The track filter button helps you to find tracks that are either related in key, a similar BPM or a similar rating of energy level. For example you could set it for everything in a related key plus or minus a certain bpm. This is a feature that you must setup first with Rekordbox software. If you want to search for songs there is a touch screen QWERTY keyboard. Then there is a tag list which is where you can tag tracks and dump them into a playlist whilst you're playing. This helps to remind yourself that you want to play them a bit later. The touchpad allows you to jump around the track and skip wherever you want to. If you hold down menu this is the utility where all of the settings are for various different system preferences.

When you select a track you will see the waveform which you can zoom in on and also edit it's grid settings. If a song is off the grid adjust it here to ensure your mixes stay locked in. At the top of the screen is a phase meter which is a visual reference for how the songs you are mixing match up on the grid. There are two options, one shows the beats in blocks and another shows parallel waveforms with transients. Using this reference you can see if the songs you are mixing are out of phase.

In the middle of the player is a large jog wheel for controlling the song, speed and direction. The response rate can be adjusted using the jog adjustment dial on the right. Above the jog wheel you can set up loops. There is a button here which is a for an instant eight bar loop. Press it once and it puts you straight into loop mode. If you press it whilst it's looping it will cut the loop down by a half each time. This is really cool for making build ups. There is also a loop mode next to that where you can set the start and end points of a manual loop.

On the right side of the CDJ you have disc eject for CDs. Below that is vinyl speed adjust for break and release. This determines what happens when pressing stop and start. If you have it set short it will be normal but longer settings will create a slow pitched down effect similar to how old school turntables behave. Next you have a mode for Vinyl or CD, this depends on your preferences. Vinyl is better if you want to use the jog wheel more for scratching and dropping in hip hop style. Whilst CD mode is better for continuous mixing such as with house or techno.

Next you have the Master and Sync buttons which can be used to lock your mixes together. When active, one CDJ acts as the master for tempo. This would be the CDJ that is currently playing through the speakers. The other CDJ you would be cueing up would be clicked to be in sync with the master. This will lock it to the tempo of the master and make your mixes really tight and on point. However if you have not set your songs properly onto the grid then it might not lock in properly. Always trust your ears first.

Finally we have the tempo fader to speed up or slow down playback. Use this to match bpm with the song you are mixing into. If you need more variation in speed you can increase its depth with the +-6 to - wide button. If you activate the Master tempo button then the pitch won't be affected by it. However if you want some cool effects, turn it off and use a wide tempo to create a really speeded up or super slowed down sound. The tempo reset button on the right will bring the speed back to default zero.

DJM900 Nexus

The DJM900 Nexus is an industry standard mixer that will probably be around for the next five years. It is easy to understand and very reliable.

On the top left side are two inputs for laptops. If your DJing with a laptop it allows you to easily plug in here without having to worry about a soundcard or audio interface. Below this are two microphone controls with gain, high and low eq potentiometers. Having these is great if you work with an mc because you can both have instant control at your fingertips.

The mixer features four identical channels each with gain, three band eq, color knob, cue button and x fader controls. The x fader is the most commonly used for transitions. You can assign how slow or fast it acts by using the switch on the right side of the mixer. Quick fades are great for hip hop mixing whilst slower ones work well with house or techno. If you really like to cut in and out quickly you can use the crossfader located at the bottom of the mixer. Each channel can be assigned to be A or B or Thru. Typically you would assign them to be Thru so that they are on their standard numerical assignment. If you want to use the crossfader assign them to the A or B side of the crossfader.

There are six different sound color fx which are available by using the sound color knob assigned to each of the four channels. These include, space, dub echo, gate/comp, noise, crush and filter. Add these to your transitions by sweeping them in and out to create really cool transitions. Below the sound color fx are the headphone controls. You can mix the source with the cue channel and control volume for headphones. If you want to listen to a channel just press its cue button.

On the right side of the mixer is the master gain, left and right balance, mono/stereo switch and booth monitor gain. This is used to directly control the volume of the booth monitor. In a club or festival setup there will often be a delay between the live feed and the monitor. Make sure you can hear the monitor clearly but without damaging your ears. Below the monitor control are the intensity curve settings for the eq, x faders and cross fader. Set these depending on your mixing style.

On the far right of the mixer is the beat effects section. You can assign effects including, delay, echo, ping pong, spiral,

spiral, reverb, trans, filter, flanger, phaser, pitch, slip roll, roll, vinyl brake, helix to each of the channels, microphone, or master mix. Below you can adjust the timing so that effects are occurring quicker or slower. You could for example have a quick scattered delay or a long echo. Or you could have a very sudden trans effect where it seems like the music suddenly stops like on a record deck. Or you could make it longer as if it is being switched off. Then you have the intensity knob for the effects and also an on/off button for them. This is great if you want to suddenly turn on an effect such as a quick LFO filter. Or a dramatic flange over a transition. On newer versions of the mixer there are buttons to cut the low, mid and high frequencies of effects. I recommend leaving the low cut so that you don't get too much interference of low frequencies.

Laptop DJ

Some DJ's prefer working with a laptop when mixing. The advantage to this is you can hold a lot more music and generally access it a lot more quickly and easily. It is debatable that sound quality degrades when using a laptop since the sound has been processed more. It is also important to note that using a laptop may distance you from the crowd a bit more since you would be looking at a screen most of the time. When mixing with a USB your more visual and engaged with the crowd. However if you decide to work with a laptop then the best option is to use Serato. This is a DJ software allowing you to manage and play your music library with CDJ's and a DJ mixer or a controller. Normally this can be set up by using an audio interface such as a Rane D/A Box that will connect your computer straight to the CDJ and DJ mixer. On some DJ mixers you can plug your laptop straight in.

USB

Nowadays the majority of DJ's are playing from USB. It's possible to also use SD cards with newer CDJ's but for the majority USB is more popular in addition to being quicker and handling larger sizes for a more affordable price.

To make sure you get the best performance for your money you need to know what specifications actually matter. Storage capacity is something that needs to be decided by the individual but 32 gig is a good start. Next you want to pay specific attention to read speed and write speed. The USB 2.0 specification is 60 megabytes per second and the USB 3.0 is 640 megabytes per second. Keep in mind though that these are just theoretical and each drive is going to have its own speed that is probably a whole lot slower. Speed can help the players feel more snappy when it comes to browsing and searching for tracks and is hugely important if you don't want to spend hours waiting for your files to transfer from your software. Therefore USB 3 is the best to go with. Kingston, The Corsair Survivor range and GTX models are all great brands/models. If you find a USB that you like, buy a couple more because if stuff gets lost or broken you need to be able to keep the party going. In addition, make sure you keep your USB in its own bag or compartment to keep it protected.

Where Do DJs Get Their Music?

Where you find music depends on what you need it for. For example if you are playing a wedding, you will get music from a different place than if your playing at a club.

Many DJ's these days rip music from YouTube. **I would not recommend this.** If you're getting songs off YouTube what you're doing is you're getting it from the music videos. Sometimes in music videos, the music will stop or there might be live action sound effects or dialogue on the top. In addition music logo's might be played on the top such as the infamous- Hardwell On Air logo. If you rip music straight from YouTube you will get those sound effects in the song. This is going to make you look stupid if you play it out, believe me I have seen it. The other reason is the quality is low. Quality wise you should use at least MP3 320 kbps, WAV or AAC.

The first place to find music is iTunes. If you have a song in mind and you want it quickly then you can get a high quality download there. Generally iTunes is best for pop music. If you are looking for more specific genres then Beatport is great. There are so many genres on there and you can tune into to the tastes of each genre with charts by DJ's and charts of sales. Beatport gives you additional information like the beats per minute (bpm) of the song and what key it is in. It is really easy to use and you can sign up for a free account.

The next source I recommend is DJ pools. Now if you're not familiar with the concept of the DJ pool, it's a place where DJs can get access to new music. Back in the vinyl days when record companies would plan a new release they would first press a limited amount of copies on vinyl. They would then distribute those copies among the DJ's so they could start playing it in the clubs, the radio or on mixtapes to promote it. Nowadays DJ pools have moved online and you can become a member. Most of them do require a monthly fee but you get unlimited access to a lot of music for around $20 per month. DJ pools also make special edits of songs or improve on them. DJ city is my favorite.

I also recommend you subscribe to a bunch of YouTube channels whose music you like so that whenever they have new releases you can be notified. www.souncloud.com is good too, you can find some cool, edits and unreleased things there. Just search around. Then also www.hypeddit.com is great for downloading mashup packs. If your a commercial DJ keep an eye on the trends through Billboard charts and also Shazam is cool if you hear a song you like, then it can identify it.

How to Understand Genres

Afro House
118 to 124 bpm
beat driven 4/4 music with lots of strong percussion samples and latin vocals.
popular in south africa

Prominent Artists Include
Black Coffee, Black Motion, Darque, Bucie, Da Capo, Sir LSG, Tumelo, Lilac Jeans, Jullian Gomes, Derrick Flair, DJ Afrozilla.

Big Room

128 - 132 bpm
4/4 dance floor music with big synths and big bass kicks. Popular in most large commercial clubs and festivals

Prominent Artists Include
Hardwell, Madig, Basshackers, MAKJ, Wolfpack, KSHMR, Nervo, R3hab, Dimitri Vegas and Like Mike, Martin Garrix

Breaks
120 - 130 bpm
4/4 Sample driven music with heavy live breakbeats and big baselines. Popular in USA and UK, underground clubs.

Prominent Artists Include
Plump DJs, Freestylers, Justin Martin, Stanton Warriors

Dance
122- 128 bpm
4/4 commercial sound with catchy vocal hooks or melodies over tight drums and a strong kick.

Prominent Artists Include
Tiesto, Calvin Harris, Alok, Martin Solvet, Madison Mars, Mike Cervello, Vintage Culture, Brohug

Deep House
120 - 124 bpm

4/4 simple sounds and longer transitions with lots of ambience and light textures. Popular at bars, rooftops and in the UK.

Prominent Artists Include
Audiojack, Kassian, Musumeci, Donatello, Kaz James, Matthias Meyer, Stereocalypse

Drum and Bass
172-175 bpm

High energy music with rolling drums and big basslines. Some songs are more atmospheric but most aimed at the dance floor. popular in the UK.

Prominent Artists Include
Andy C, Chase and Status, Sub Focus, TC, Rene Lavice, Loadstar, Cyantific, Mampi Swift,

Dubstep
140 - 155 bpm

Screechy sounds, huge drops, big bass and hard drums. Often features samples and catchy hooks. Popular in The USA and at festivals.

Prominent Artists Include
Zombie, Datsic, Skrillex, Virtual Riot, Wooli, Herobust, Tynan,

Electro House
126 - 128 bpm

Big beats, hard sounds, synth leads and basslines. Often very technical and high energy with lots of samples and short sounds. Popular in clubs.

Prominent Artists Include
Joyride, Curbi, Dyro, Brohug, Bingo players, Krunk, Uberjackd, Chocolate Puma,

Electronica/Downtempo

100 - 124 bpm

Electronic/synthetic minimal sounds over slowed down house style beats. Some songs feature samples but synthetic sounds are more common. Works well at lounges and bars. Popular in Europe.

Prominent Artists Include
Bicep, Andreas Balicri, Sascha Kawa, Zuma Dionys, Mariel Ito, Timboletti, Serken Eles, Valeron

Funk, Soul, Disco
118 - 126 bpm

Heavily influenced by or sampling 70's funk, disco and soul music. Played over house 4/4 kick drum driven beats. Popular in gay clubs and USA.

Prominent Artists Include
Purple House, Joey Negro, Disco Incorporated, Funk The Beat, Thedjlawyer, Dimitri from Paris

Funky, Groove, Jackin House
120 -126 bpm

Samples and draws influence from classic disco and house records with a more updated and current sound. Works well as a warm up in commercial clubs.

Prominent Artists Include
DOD, Block and Crown, Richard Grey, Scotty Boy, Antoine Clamaran, Lissat, Agua Sin Gas, Basement Jaxx,

Future House

124 - 128 bpm

Big melodies using lots of strong sounds combined with hard hitting kicks and big build ups. Popular at festivals and commercial clubs.

Prominent Artists Include
Don Diablo, Mesto, Martin Garrix, Justin Mylo, Malaa, Mr Belt and Wezol, Steffi de campo, Swanky Tunes

Garage / Bassline / Grime
128 - 134 bpm

4/4 beats with a lot of swing. Wobbly basslines, stabs and some dark atmospherics. Some songs are more uplifting and funky, drawing inspiration from older styles. Popular in The UK and underground clubs.

Prominent Artists Include
My nu leng, Le Duke, Volac, DustyCloud, Phlegmatic Dogs, Ac Slater, Dram, Amber Mark, DJ EZ,

Glitch Hop
90 - 110 bpm

Big beats, with samples or processed effects. Very similar to hip hop or slowed down trap and breaks. Works well with dancing shows or in some small hip hop clubs.

Prominent Artists Include
Alias, K Lab, Staunch, Thomas Vent, Fort Knox, Grid Division, Popular Alive.

Hard Dance

150 - 160 bpm

Hard hitting beats, primarily driven by a big distorted kick and bassline. Big synth melodies or off beat bass lines and samples combine with the kick. Popular at festivals.

Prominent Artists Include
Headhunterz, Coone, TNT, Showtek, Technoboy, Darren Styles, D-Block, Timmy Trumpet, Brennan Hart, Ran D.

Hardcore and Hard Techno
126 - 130 bpm

Minimal arrangements with hard hitting sounds and attenuated melodies. Very dark and hypnotic. Works well at warehouse parties and underground European clubs.

Prominent Artists Include
T78, Pomela, Goncalo, Helldriver, Alberto Ruiz, ABBYVSM, Angy Kore, Oliver emmer, deker.

Hardcore and Hard Techno
126 - 130 bpm

Minimal arrangements with hard hitting sounds and attenuated melodies. Very dark and hypnotic. Works well at warehouse parties and underground European clubs.

Prominent Artists Include
T78, Pomela, Goncalo, Helldriver, Alberto Ruiz, ABBYVSM, Angy Kore, Oliver emmer, deker.
Hip Hop and R and B
70 - 160 bpm

Beats, rhymes and life. Most songs based around a vocal, either singing or rapping. Complimented by tight beats and cool melodies or sampling. Popular in most mainstream clubs in Western countries.

Prominent Artists Include
Drake, Rihanna, Beyonce, Kanye West, Post Malone, The Weeknd, Travis Scott, Arrianna Grande, Nicki Minaj.

House
126 - 130 bpm

4/4 driven by a consistent kick. Typically arranged with intro, break down then sixty four bars of drop. Very formulaic and designed for DJ's. Uses vocals, strong melodies and basslines. Works well as a warm up at most clubs or day time parties.

Prominent Artists Include
David Guetta, Bob Sinclair, Oliver Heldens, Natema, Riva Starr, David Penn, Paul Woolford, Josh Butler, Dennis Cruz, Leon.

Indie Disco / Nu Disco
110 - 124 bpm

Modern synthetic sounds played in a way that is similar to seventies disco and funk. Big electronic beats and catchy synth patterns. Works well as a background music.

Prominent Artists Include
Younger rebinds, Throttle, Kungs, Purple Disco Machine, Red Axes, L'imperatrice, Showbiz, Yuksek

Leftfield Bass
75 - 150 bpm

An alternative take on more popular bass driven genres such as house, trap and hip hop. Using different patterns or more experimental sounds. Works well for listening at home or mixtapes.

Prominent Artists Include
G-Rex, Peekaboo Wakaan, Nocturnal Sunshine, OAKK, DNA, An-ten-nae, ENiGMA Dubz, G Jones, Liquid Stranger, Dean Biscuit

Melodic House and Techno
120 - 124 bpm

4/4 Designed for DJ music. Long and progressive arrangements with kick leading and luscious melodies and bass play in symphony. Popular in European style clubs.

Prominent Artists Include
Guy Gerber, Maceo Plex, Adam Port, OC & Verde, Kolsch, Hale Bopp, Sasha, La Fleur

Minimal / Deep Tech
122 - 127 bpm

4/4 driven by a consistent kick and designed for DJ mixing. Simple melodies, clean drums. Hypnotic rhythms and long progressive development. Popular in European style clubs.

Prominent Artists Include
Low Rich, Stephan Bazbaz, Arkady Antsyrev, Archie Hamilton, Benson Herbert, Luuk Van Dijk, James Dexter, Nick Curly

Progressive House
126 - 128 bpm

Features beautiful melodies and breakdowns that build up to euphoric drops. Drops are driven by a kick, bass and typically a nice synthetic lead. Works well at festivals and clubs.

Prominent Artists Include
Alesso, Calvin Harris, Armin Van Burren, Thomas Gold, Borgeous, KSHMR, Dannic, Dirty Vegas, Avicii, Swedish House Mafia

PsyTrance
138 - 144 bpm

Bass heavy music usually constructed in a staccato stuttering fashion formed around a 4/4 kick drum. Synthetic fx and rhythmic melodies play over the top. Arrangements are long and progressive. Works well at festivals and in some open format sets.

Prominent Artists Include
Armin Van Burren, Vini Vici, Timmy Trumpet, Sphera, Outsiders, Protonica, Ace Ventura, Captain Hook, Gaudium, Animato, Stryker,
Reggae / Dance Hall / Dub
80 - 160 bpm

Most songs feature a vocal as the focus, usually a singer or some samples. Offbeat snare and percussion make up the beats. Bass lines and licks of instruments gel together in the mix. Works well played in live environments.

Prominent Artists Include
Joseph Cotton, Shy FX, Kiko Bun, Kalibwoy, Finest Sno, Darr3n Afreaka, Era Istrefi, Walshy Fire, Kalibandulu, Blaiz Fayah, Richie Loop

Tech House
120 -126 bpm

4/4 driven by a consistent kick. Very formulaic and designed for DJ's. Usually features the kick and a driving bassline as the main features. Some samples and simple melodies come in and out. Popular in underground clubs.

Prominent Artists Include
Tim Baresko, Shiba San, Green Velvet, Chris Lake, Dom Dolla, Eskuche, Solardo Sola, Mason Maynard, Pornographic

Techno
126 - 128 bpm

Very industrial sound with a kick and minimal instruments. Typically a kick and bassline with some samples or simple melodies. Arrangements are long and hypnotic, building up and breaking down. Popular for warehouse parties and European clubs.

Prominent Artists Include
Carl Cox, Thomas Schumacher, Victor Ruiz, Adam Beyer, Bart Skils, UMEK, Kraftek, Radio Slave, SRVD, Patrick Mason, P.leone

Trance
134 - 138 bpm

Usually features a vocal or huge melody as the main focus. All about creating a very euphoric build up to a harmony of sound. Long and progressive arrangements. Works well at festivals and niche club nights.

Prominent Artists Include
Josie Giuseppe, John O'Callaghan, James Dymond , Factor B, Yotto, Armin van Buuren, Darren Porter, Paul Denton, Craig Connelly

Trap / Future Bass
140 - 150 bpm

Trap is all about hard hitting beats and bass with powerful 808 kick drums arranged to create a breathing in and out slamming and snappy arrangement complimented by big sounds and tight leads. Future bass is more musical with layered complex leads and lush musical arrangements.

Prominent Artists Include
Herobust, Chainsmokers, Flume, Illenium, Saymyname, DJ Snake, Nitti Gritti, Habstrakt, RL Grime, Diplo, Jack U, Aazar.

How To Organize And Manage Your Music

Rekordbox

Rekordbox is a software for organizing your music library in preparation for use with Pioneer CDJ's. Before you start importing your music files into it you must make sure your files are not all over the place because if you ever change computers Rekordbox isn't going to know where to find the files. What I suggest is to create folders for each month of the year and put your latest downloads in there and then import them into Rekordbox to organize.

When you import new music you can analyze the songs to get relevant information such as bpm and length. There are two analyze settings, normal and dynamic. Normal is for electronic music that has a really consistent beat and dynamic is for music that may have fluctuations in the BPM such as live music or mash ups with tempo changes. if you import music that you know has tempo changes be sure to analyze with the dynamic mode. Then there's two analisis modes, normal and performance. The default is set to normal and basically what normal mode will do is not use too much CPU power when importing and analyzing tracks. If your DJing with Rekordbox on in the background, use this mode so that your computer won't eat up too much brain power. However if you want analysis to complete as quickly as possible it's worth setting it to the performance mode.

To import music you can drag and drop it into a new playlist. Rekordbox will then analyze the songs and then the waveform will appear. When you have imported music there might be duplicate entries. Rekordbox doesn't have a way to remove duplicate tracks inside a collection and the reason is because they're not actually duplicate entries they're referencing different music files. This is a symptom if your music is a absolute mess. Maybe it's because you've copied the same music file to a different location on your hard drive and you've imported both of them. Basically it ends up where you've got the same song or two copies of the file in different places on your computer. There's no way that Rekordbox can automatically determine that these files are actually called the same things. You can either delete the source file or go through your collection and click remove from collection.

Now that we've removed duplicates from our collection we're ready to create playlists. Playlists are logical groupings of music that allow you to better organize your collection and prepare for a gig. Clicking on the playlist tab will reveal a little plus to create a new playlist and it will ask you to name it. You can call playlists whatever you want as long as it makes sense to you. What I normally do is name them by genre. You can also create folders for multiple playlists. This is a good idea if you are playing lot's of different types of gigs. You could have one set in a folder with playlists and then another and so on. To add music to these playlists all you need to do is basically collect the tracks you want to add to the playlist, then drag and drop them into the playlist. You can also add tags to songs for labeling them in different genres or moods or energy, whatever you want. When you use the track filter setting on the CDJ clicking it will display this amazing menu where you can select to display by the tabs you have set up.

When your ready to export this music to a USB key or SD card for use in Pioneer DJ gear, simply insert the USB into your computer. You can see that it appears under the devices window within Rekordbox. Click Sync manager at the bottom of the screen which will bring up a display of three panels, iTunes, Rekordbox and your device. Clicking on a collection will essentially select the tracks to put on a USB key and drag that over to it's window. Or click the box of the lists that you want to export to your USB then click the arrow across. Exporting can take a little while and of course that all depends on the quality of the USB. When it is done, make sure the Rekordbox database has been finalized and then click on the little USB eject icon. You can then insert that USB into a CDJ supporting Rekordbox and your collection of playlists, settings and folder will appear on the CDJ in exactly the same way.

Mixed In Key

The perfect mix, doesn't just come down to beat matching, it also comes down to song selection and usually choosing two songs that are either in the same key or in similar keys. When talking about the keys of songs things can quickly turn very technical and you can just go down a rabbit hole of technicalities. If you are a complete beginner all you need to know is that all music is written in certain keys. You get major keys and minor keys. There's a few other keys as well but you don't need to worry about them. There are certain keys that go really well together and certain keys that just completely clash with each other. If you want to get that perfect mix it's better to blend keys in that go well with each other. The most reliable technique will be mixing songs that are in the exact same key or a closely related one.

Mixed in Key is a very useful tool to analyze tracks for key, tempo and energy level of a song. Within the software you can then add cue points and all data will be written into the metadata of the file which is in turn displayed in Rekordbox, Serato or whatever DJ software you use. There is also a piano keyboard so you can check the key by playing the root note to decide whether you think it's got it right.

Mixed in Key organizes musical keys using the Camelot system. The Camelot wheel is a system used to mix your music harmonically without having to memorize all the keys. When you first look at the Camelot wheel you'll notice it looks almost exactly like the circle of fifths with twelve key steps around the circle and each of those keys being a fifth step from the last. The key positions on the Camelot wheel are rotated five steps counterclockwise. Each key in the Camelot wheel is assigned an alphanumeric code ranging from 1 to 12. On the outer circle of the wheel are major keys and the inner circle are the relative minor key. Major keys are always labeled with the number and the letter B and the minor keys are always labeled with a number and the letter A.

Think of the numbers on the Camelot wheel like the hours on a clock.

To create harmonically pleasing mixes you can move around the wheel one step up or down, clockwise or counterclockwise while staying within the same ring. Each number represents a step up or down from the previous number. If you go forward or backward one step or within the same number then you'll have a harmonically compatible mix. Just be sure to stick with the same letter which just means that you're staying in the same ring of the wheel. There are some cool things you can utilize with this, maybe you to give some energy to a mix. Simply, step up the number clockwise to move to the next key like moving from 3A to 4A. The shift creates a lift in energy because you will be mixing into a key that is a fifth higher than the current key. Alternatively you can lower the energy on the dance floor slightly by going down a step counterclockwise such as mixing from for 3A to 2A. However that depends on the song you're mixing. For instance if you're mixing high energy songs when you go down a step it can actually create a unique effect of taking your audience deeper into your mix which creates a cool contrast to help you stand out as a DJ.

Some argue that you might lose creativity relying on Mixed In Key because you might ignore songs that aren't in the same key range resulting in missed opportunities in your mix. The bottom line is that it is not a hard and fast rule. Once you understand the system and your ears get more sensitive to the key signatures in regards to what melds and what doesn't then you can get creative and experiment. You will have intuitively trained your ear to be able to identify whole sections of music that are compatible with each other from different songs and you won't end up with any dissonant surprises. If you do get any key clashes at least you'll know it and won't play those songs together ever again.

Serato

Serato is a DJ software that enables you to organize and playback music with CDJ's or a controller. It is a pretty simple software as far as layout is concerned. It can be basically broken up into into two to three sections. First there is a deck section where the actual DJing happens. There are three modes offered for the decks. You have absolute mode which treats it more like a normal CD or vinyl. You have relative mode where you get access to things like cue points which you don't get in an absolute mode. Then you have your internal mode which actually bypasses the DVS part of Serato so instead of playing through the CDs or vinyl it's just playing straight through the computer and you don't have any physical control over it. There are upto four decks available, depending on how many decks you want to be playing. The deck overview shows you the song's bpm, time elapsed and the time remaining. To the right is the pitch percentage so when your mixing you can see how far plus or minus percentage you move the pitch. Each deck has upto six cue points available as well as loops from 1/32 to 16/1 timings.

Next is the library section and then to the right there is the playlists section. In addition there are other panels which you can open up to find files and there is also a prepare section below that. This is where you can hold songs that you might want to play next and you can simply drag songs in there. The history section allows you to actually look up what you played in the past. Maybe you had a couple songs that went really well together that you played the night before but you don't remember them off the top of your head. Serato saves all that information and puts them in order for you.

You can customize Serato into different layouts. The vertical layout which features the two decks side by side. The horizontal layout which puts the two decks on top of each other. Then finally, the extended layout which extends out the wave form even further and keeps a horizontal view. For beginners I would recommend the vertical view because it makes the most sense visually on the software. When you look down at your controller or your turntables or your CDJs it makes sense because it kind of mirrors where you have the song.

Traktor

Traktor is a DJ software that can be used to interface between a computer and a controller or a DJ mixer with two CDJs set up. Some controllers are made exclusively for use with Traktor.

When it comes to loading music into the software there are number ways to do it. You can load music from the computer hard drive or from an external source. If you want to use an external source ensure that is connected to your computer before you start Traktor otherwise it might not read it properly. Lastly you can add your iTunes playlists into it. Whatever you decide to use simply drag the music files from there location or right click import to collection and then place them in the relevant playlist or folder inside of Traktor. Like other music management software it is wise to keep files well organized on your computer.

Traktor automatically analyzes imported songs and can work out their length and BPM. You can analyze songs automatically one by one or if you're doing a batch, you can right-click on the playlist folder or track collection and select analyze. Make sure you don't do this when your about to perform as this will be an issue. If you have lots of tracks you need to analyze then make sure you run them when you have time to leave the computer, for example overnight.

After analysis Traktor will create a waveform and if you have the auto gain feature on it will set it so that you have similar amplitudes of songs. Finally it will set the song to a beat grid allowing you to mix in time. If necessary you can adjust this to get the timing of the track correct. If you want to use a sync function on your mixes then locking your songs to the grid is essential.

The track collection is basically your music library with all the songs, playlist and folders that you set up. There is an information window for your songs. The first column shows symbols and letters to give you information about the current song. For example a tick means you've already played it and an exclamation mark indicates that Traktor cannot find it. If this happens you can right click and relocate it or delete it from the collection. You can organize the collection however you want. For example by, title, artist, BPM, time, key and genre

Cue points can easily be created in Traktor. Typically you would place them at important parts of the song such as the first beat or the breakdown. When you press the cue it will continue playing from that point and if the song is not playing then it won't start the song but it will jump to that cue point. You can also add loops into the song and there is also an option to set a fade in and out marker. When it hits the fade-out it will automatically start the next track.

How to Mix Like a Pro

Theory

Right so now you have your knowledge, equipment and your set is ready. Let's start mixing. Wait, before you start mixing you first have to know a little bit about music theory. Hey, don't get scared! It's not that hard, it's all about counting to four. The basics you need to know are about bars. A bar or measure is made up of a group of beats that you can count so that you know where you are in the song. Music is written on a series of horizontal lines called a staff. A vertical line drawn through the staff is called a bar line. The bar is the space between two bar lines where the beats are grouped together. Notes are symbols that define how long a sound lasts. There are different kinds of notes and they all relate to each other. Mathematically the longest sounding note is the whole note. It lasts for four beats and you can only have one whole note in a bar. A little fraction code at the beginning of the staff is called the time signature and that tells you how to count the beats. The majority of club music is in 4/4 time. This means that there are four beats in every bar. The top number in the fraction represents the number of beats to count in each bar, which is four beats. The bottom number indicates which type of note receives one beat/count and in this signature it's the quarter note. Think of it like a dollar bill with one dollar being the whole note and four, twenty five cent quarters representing the quarter notes. Since one bar is four beats we count it one, two, three, four.

Standard Mixing

The standard mix is whilst a song is playing out of the main speakers you would have another song cued in your headphones.

First you select your cue point which you would have already set in Rekordbox. Usually it's the very first kick of the song. Whenever you press the cue or hot cue button you will hear it. Check the loudness of both songs to ensure they are equally loud. You can also use the metering on the mixer to help.

Next, match the BPM to the song you are mixing into. Now it's all about waiting for the right point in time to drop in. Tap with your feet or count one, two, three, four until your song playing out comes to a new measure. Typically in dance music its after four measures. With the fader down of the song in your headphones press the cue to start it. Depending on how fast your response is you will either have started at exactly the right time or you will be slower or faster then the song playing. If one of them is faster or slower it will sound horrible. You have to adjust by ear to lock them into each other. If it ever happens that they are not in sync anymore you can just push the jog wheel a little in the right direction. Make sure you always count to four and make sure that the beats are on top of each other. If you ever had piano lessons you know exactly how to put them on top of eachother.

But matching those two songs is not everything. The mixer in the middle allows you to mix between both sources. The song playing out of the speakers on one channel and the song in your headphones on another channel. Once they are locked in you can start to bring the fader up and fade one in whilst fading the other out. That's the most basic transition fading in one song and fading out the other one while retaining the beat matching.

It can be really easy to fall into the trap of mixing in and out the same way every time. Now there's nothing wrong with this but you can start to make your set sound quite predictable. Following on are some cool more advanced, mixing techniques.

Bass Cut

The next technique would be to actually do the same just a little bit more refined. What I love to do is mix in a song with the bass frequencies cut. You can use the low eq knob for this. I just kill it and after a few bars turn the bass of the new song in and cut the bass of the other one. It's like your switching the basslines up. This sounds awesome on most dance music since it is bass driven. Sometimes I leave the gap and just turn it all on suddenly, so the people feel the bass kicking in again. You can just kill the bass for four bars kick it back in again and get the people really excited

Mixing With Sound Color FX

There's of course a lot more advanced stuff you can do. For example you can use the mixers sound color effects. First you select them and control them with the knobs on each channel. When they're in the middle position they're off and then you can either turn them down or up. Try using the filter to sweep a song out. Try the echo to scatter the beats out. Space is really cool to make the mix go distant and wide. Use the noise filter to add drama to build ups.

Mixing With Beat FX

The beat fx section is awesome for creating unique mixes or for smoothing out transitions. Some of my personal favorites are the flange, phaser, beat rolls and delay. Flange I often apply towards the end of a transition or to suddenly bring in a mix. I set it to be a long slow flange and then sweep the wet/dry mix to around fifty percent or more. Make sure you cut the low frequencies or mix over a break that has less lower frequencies because flange can really exaggerate the low end. For a more audible and crazier version of this use the phaser. Delay is great if you are switching tempos or stop the music. You can make the stop less abrupt by scattering over a little bit of delay. Beat rolls are great to use as a build up on songs.

Filter In and Out

Using the filters is a great way to smoothly reveal a new song. To start, make sure the filter of the song playing out of the speakers is turned off/in the middle default. The song cued in your headphones should have the filter knob turned all the way up. This is for a high pass sweep. You can adjust how extreme the sweep is with the color fx master knob. Slowly sweep the cued song in whilst sweeping the main song out. It will create a really cool and smooth mix.

Vinyl Stop/Drop In

The CDJ's have a setting for how quickly or slowly the playback starts and stops. It is on the right hand side. If you set it slow then when you press play/pause you get these long stops where the music slows down. Try setting it about twenty five percent and when your ready hit the play/pause button. This would be at the end of one song and at the same time or a little later, you press play for the other CDJ. That one should be a more instant start. It's a really clean way to mix two different songs and works well if your changing BPM. Another more extreme way is to set the tempo fader to wide. Then turn off key lock so that the pitch will follow the adjustments. Normally at the end of the night or at the end of the last DJ's set I would slowly, slow down the music to let the audience be aware of the change coming. Add some delay over the top to make it sound more pleasing.

Backspin

At the end of your transitions you can quickly spin back the song your mixing out. It's like a fast rewind effect. Be careful though, the back spin can sound quite loud and abrupt if not done properly so make sure the level is right and the low frequencies are cut.

Loop

On Pioneer CDJ's you can easily activate a four beat loop with one button. I like to add this on a longer transition. You could loop some phrase or melody whilst mixing the other song in. Then press the loop button again and again to speed up the loop and turn it into a roll. This is great for creating your own build ups and making mixes more exciting.

Mashing Things Up

Mashups will help you stand out as a unique DJ. Essentially they are combining different parts of songs that you like into one composite song. You might be thinking that's a remix. But they're different from a remix because the remix is when you take one song and put a different feel to that same song. A mashup is when you actually take two or more completely different songs and you put them together.

There are a few different ways to choose songs for a mash up. You can pick a theme such as, folk music, or pop music. Sometimes people like to pick artists and choose two different songs by the same artist. Sometimes people choose an older artist and a newer artist to show that the two artists are very similar. For instance you might pair a Bruno Mars song with a Michael Jackson song just to showcase how their songwriting styles are so similar. The best way is to listen to one song and then try to sing another song at the same time. If you can do that then that has the makings for a great mashup. Mixed In Key is great for this because you can easily identify songs that will work well together based on their key. Usually you would mash up songs in the same key or the next harmonic key. It's also important to have the same bpm but if its not then you can speed it up or slow it down in your editing software.

Mashups for DJ's often feature a vocal only (acapella) from another song on the break down of a different song. You could for example take a classic breakdown and mash it up with a newer drop. In other more advanced cases you can blend bpms. Say for example you are going from 128 bpm big room to 150 bpm trap. You could get two songs in the same key, edit where you want them to blend and then apply a tempo stretch in your editing software. This will help a lot when playing out live since you can effortlessly go from one genre to the next.

In addition to mash ups you should check over all of your songs before you play them out. Sometimes they might have parts you don't like that are too long or maybe need a better build up to keep the dancefloor energy. Edit these in or out using any digital audio workstation and then export to your music management software of choice.

How to Get Gigs

Before you start looking for gigs you need to make sure your skills are as tight as can be and that your library is lit. Get feedback on them, record mixes and ensure all is good to go. When you are ready to start hustling, start letting everyone know that you're a DJ. Not just on Instagram. Let any people you come across know that your DJ. I get calls all the time asking for me to DJ at a party. Sometimes they don't even know how good I am, but they just know that I'm a DJ. If you don't feel like going up to people and talking to them personally, you can hit them up on Instagram Twitter, Facebook, or whatever. It's all about getting the word out.

The next thing you should do is to check out if your area has online pages or profiles that promote parties. Search Google, Facebook and Instagram for your city + parties. Visit them and direct message them asking if they need a DJ. At the start you're probably going to DJ for free a lot which is alright because you'll be getting a lot of experience.

Another thing you can do is become a part of your DJ community. This involves meeting other DJ's and regularly hanging out with them. It can open up a lot of doors for you. I have met some DJ's hanging out a club and then of course our mutual interests form a bond. It's given me so much value, from being able to play at massive festivals to the hottest clubs. You definitely want to be a part of the DJ community. Find a mentor or a local DJ that you see gigging every weekend. Try to hang out with them as much as possible. Go see their shows, attend their workshops, whatever you can do to be around them. If you have a few remixes, mashups or your own songs share them. They might think this dude really has some good music and they'll help put you on one day. You can even tell that same local DJ that if you ever need a DJ to come open up for you then you will be available. Or if you are ever running late and you want me to connect the equipment, let me know I can come do that for you for free. If you do a good job and the promoter and the club owners notice it they're going to say let's bring this DJ back again.

Make connections with companies that host events. Before you hit up these event companies you want to make sure that you're active on social media. Post content so it shows that you're legit DJ and not one who is going to show up and suck. An easy way to make content is to bring a friend to the parties with you and have them take pictures and videos of you. Once you've been getting more gigs and building up your social profile you can start reaching out to event groups and clubs. Search places on Instagram and look up a venue that you know hosts events or parties. Look for fliers, pictures or videos posted by DJs and then here you'll find like an event company logo at the top. You can then go to their page and direct message them saying something like, I want to DJ for you guys what can I do to make this happen? Build relationships with them, find out what they are looking for and understand their needs. When you message these event companies make sure to tell them that you have friends that will come because they love when you bring people to their events.

Go to clubs where the music is played that you love. Write down the top five clubs, bars and lounges that you want to go DJ at. Visit them and ask to speak with the owner or manager. Introduce yourself as a DJ who is interested to perform there. Most times you will get a positive reaction since they are hit up on social media and online so much that meeting people face to face shows value and initiative. If you have a mix ready that really fits the style of the club pass it to them. In fact make a bunch of mixes. Do not aim the mixtape to the peak time of the club as it is more likely that you will play at the beginning or the end. Also don't expect to get paid so don't ask for payment. As previously mentioned at the start this is very unlikely. Be happy that you're able to play in front of people, if you are lucky you will get a couple of guestlist places and maybe some free drinks. But be warned, don't overdo it with the free drinks as this can go horribly wrong.

Management

At some point when the demands meet it, you might need management. They should support you, have a strategy for you, develop you as an artist and help you to jumpstart your career. This can involve, checking emails, getting in contact with labels, taking care that you get paid and all these kind of things. In addition a good manager should have contacts that help you.

If you have choices, do not pick the first one. Wait until you have like four or five people that want to work with you. Meet them and try to find out what their plans are. If they have a good strategy for you, believe in you, and you feel happy with them then it could be the start of a winning relationship. If you get lucky, your manager will be really ambitious and take consistent, massive action that brings results. Ideally you want someone that is already working within the industry and can help you to get connected with other people and pitch you to labels and all these kind of things. Before you sign remember that the management is offering a service and will be getting a percentage from whatever you are making. The standard is that the management gets from fifteen to twenty five percent.

Everything above twenty five percent is just a ripoff. Don't even think about it.

Booking Agents

A booking agent is basically just like a travel agent. They will be taking care of your show dates, flights, accomodation and the negotiation for the money. The second you're so famous that people start writing you and want to book you is when you will need a booking agent.

How to get in contact with them? You can search directories or ask touring DJ's. Try and get in touch with them or make yourself so big that they want to get in touch with you. The best way is to make good music and regularly release it on the best labels.

When you work with booking agents they will often add their fees on the top. But be sure not to sell yourself short and also secure payment details upfront. Often you should be eligible for a fifty percent deposit before shows.

The fundamental key to getting bookings is relationship management. You need to be really good with people. Don't try to sell yourself too much and don't think your the best DJ. Understand what they are looking for and what they are not looking for. Get them talking about themselves and soon enough they will be curious about you and what you can offer.

Branding & Marketing

When it comes to marketing, content is king. It goes without saying but make sure that your mixing is on point because if the product sucks nobody is going to give a damn about you. Create a brand around yourself. Now when I say brand I don't mean you have to come up with some weird, wacky or wonderful DJ alias. Of course you should have a name that is cool and people remember it. But when I talk about branding I don't just mean the name you give yourself, it's about the whole package. It's about how you are perceived as a DJ and what kind of DJ you are. There are millions of DJ's out there. There are strict turntablists, resident DJ's who play regularly in clubs on a weekly basis, celebrity DJ's, mashup DJ's, producer DJ's and the list goes on. If a promoter puts you on a flyer it's not just about playing the best music anymore. You need popularity and good branding. Nowadays the popular DJ's have surpassed the talented DJ's.

How do you brand yourself as a DJ? It requires getting your name out there as much as possible. That doesn't mean spam. It's about putting yourself out there where a lot of people are going to hear about you. Connections are so important and you need to be constantly networking in the nightlife scene. It really requires being out seven nights a week. When you DJ put your brand out there, wear your logo, give out freebies with your logo on and have great visuals that show your branding. When people are taking pictures and your logo is in that picture, it is going to be circulated by the promoters of the party after the event. On top of that people are looking at the DJ booth when the party's going on. If they hear that you're playing well, then they want to see who is

DJing and they will see your logo. Put it on everything, shirts, caps, booty shorts, you name it.

You can also create DJ drops that says your DJ name so when you're in party or mixing you can play them at anytime. Get your voice heard and get your name out there. Think of your brand as your flag, you're going to hold up that flag and wave it around for people to see that flag. It should showcase what you're about. If you can design your own logo and your own website it's only going to help you as a DJ. These extra skills will help you develop a style that you can then promote. A brand doesn't come to you straight away and maybe you need to experiment. Brainstorm and map out the different parts of DJing that you enjoy. Map out the different personality traits that you have, the different nights that you like to go to and start combining some of these ideas. Come up with something that says more about you than just I'm a DJ. When you're uploading mixes think about your brand, when you're uploading pictures to social media think about your brand. Think about how you can incorporate your brand into everything that you do. Grow that brand to the biggest it can possibly be. Try not to keep changing your DJ name, avoid creating new aliases hoping that a new name is going to suddenly give you some gigs because it's not just a name that gives you a gig. It's not just one thing that gets you a gig it's the whole package. Stick with it grow it as big as you can and then I guarantee you someone, somewhere will offer you an opportunity.

Producing

It's super important nowadays for DJs to produce their own music. You only have to take a look at all the touring DJs and Top 100 DJs to see that it's mostly producers. Producing music and spreading it to everybody you know and even don't know is the key for you to be a successful DJ. Make as many tracks as it takes for you to get to where you want to be. Post your music on all your social media accounts and make sure that the right people hear it and make sure that you grow a following in the process. A word of warning though, before you publically release anything you should send it out to record labels first. They will not sign anything if it has been put out for free download before. The first step you must take is to upload your music to www.soundcloud.com as a private link. Then you can share this with labels that have similar sounds. Just search through Beatport and then find the contact information through Google searches. Labels will often take a long time to reply so be patient and don't spam them with lots of low quality music. Produce the best tracks you can and try to expose them to as many people as possible. Eventually you will build up a fanbase and at the end that's all what it's coming down to if you want to earn and DJ more.

I can't stress to you how important growing a following is. The more followers, plays, likes, shares, and views grow your chances of getting booked. Gaining more requires being creative to stand out in a crowded market. Capitalize on what you're good at and if you're good at doing those things like mixing and scratching and doing tricks then capitalize on it. Get your phone camera or video camera and record yourself doing your routine. Record yourself doing your mix and post that up on all your social media channels. When you play out or even if you are just practicing, go live on Facebook, YouTube or Instagram at least once a week. If you see a club owner or a promoter liking your video, send them a message to say thank you so much for the support and start building the business relationship. Podcast your mixes you on the radio.

Produce more content featuring, slowly and surely your numbers will justify the reasons for clubs to book you. Sometimes you might put stuff out and it gets a low response. But don't get jaded, keep pushing. DJing is such a competitive thing to do nowadays and so setting yourself apart with your uniqueness and with your numbers is key to being a successful DJ. Practice hard, make that content and don't give up. Eventually if you make enough content that gets enough traction and enough numbers then you are going to be a successful DJ. Everybody who's successful in life is successful because they showed the world their tenacity, passion and drive to succeed.

Electronic Press Kit (EPK)

When party organizers or clubs contact you they will often ask for an electronic press kit (EPK) which is essentially a DJ resume. It is so important to have a very accurate and an up to date resume that covers the look of the DJ, the genre of music they play, autobiography and insight into the highlights of their career. When it comes to creating an EPK it's really crucial you work with a group of professionals. First impressions count and bookers are going to make a decision on the nonverbal communications. They will just go on the visuals and think I don't like that dude because he didn't invest in himself or herself.

The first thing to consider is a logo. Work with a graphic designer to produce a logo that represents you. Logo's are absolutely crucial, they should be memorable, well designed and represent you. Good examples include Deadmau5, Daft Punk and Marshmello. You cannot mistake them for anybody else. Once you find something you like, stick with it and use it on all of your marketing material.

Next thing on your EPK would be the press images. Again work with a professional. Yes your friend might have a good camera. Or yes your friend might be able to take a few cool pictures with their iPhone but they won't have the technical ability to be able to do really advanced things. Professional photographers will help you stand out, utilize your best features and help choose the right locations. Their photos will usually be good for at least two years. I recommend shooting around twenty images in total. These need to be a combination of studio shot images, location shot images and profile images so that you have a real blend of looks to use. Also a combination of low key and high key images are great. For instance if you are a techno DJ the majority of your images would be more low key with a darker tone and darker clothes. If you are more of a commercial DJ then you want more colors for high key images. Your photographer should help you touch up and render your final images. Also your EPK should include the best images from your shows. Often clubs have an in house photographer so you can get those for free. If your just starting out ask a photographer to come and shoot your gig. Make sure you get one that has experience shooting in low light.

The next thing on your EPK is the biography. This would normally include, what made you want to be a DJ, what you are influenced by, what are the highlights of your career, what do you plan to do and so on. Social media links should also be included. All of the above would be created together in a PDF document that can be attached with an email. At least five to ten pages is the standard.

For example, you would have profile photo at the start with logo, then biography, some images of your shows, flyers and then social media links at the end. In addition keep a version of this on your own website. Make sure you buy a domain and hosting so that you come across as professional and legitimate as possible. If you have any videos of your shows that's great too because bookers can check out how you play.

For more ideas check out my website:

www.swindali.com

Everything You Need to Know Before You Play Your First Gig

Here are five quick tips you can use when you're doing your very first club gig.

Tip One

Be early. Don't be on time, be early. You definitely want to be professional and if it's your very first time spinning at a club, then you need that time to prepare. Especially if you are using some type of different equipment than what they're using. If you're plugging in your own stuff you definitely need that extra time to troubleshoot any problems that you might have. You will be able to handle the situation professionally, quickly and keep the night going.

Tip Two

Be professional, remember it's a business at the end of the day. You might be thinking that you're being paid to party. But at the end of the day you're offering a service and if you want to get paid and continue to get booked then be professional. Avoid getting drunk or chasing girls. Maintain a cool and friendly professional attitude at all times.

Tip Three

Lock down how you're going to get paid. if you can get a contract with the promoter or the business owner who's going to be paying you then get it in writing. Try to get a deposit which will cover you against cancellations. However in most situations you're not going to be able to do that. Sadly to say there's a lot of slack promoters out there and a lot of bad business owners who just really don't think paying a DJ is important. Be prepared for whatever may come your way. You might be put in a situation where you don't get paid. I mean definitely try to lock down how you're going to get paid and who's going to pay you and all that because it's really nice to get paid for your talent. But in the world we live in where everybody is a DJ don't be surprised if you don't get paid and don't let it affect your momentum moving forward because it often happens.

Tip Four

Make sure you have reliable equipment. If you're bringing in your own equipment to certain venues make sure it's reliable. The last thing you want is problems and the last thing you want is to cause problems for promoters or business owners. It might affect your pay and also might affect you coming back in the future. So definitely make sure that whatever you have and whatever you're going to be using is reliable, especially if it's your first time out. There are no excuses.

Tip Five

Last but not least don't be too cocky. This is really easy and can happen to a lot of DJ's especially when they're starting off and they build some momentum. The last thing you want to do is be that super cocky DJ because whoever's booking you and whoever you're going to be dealing with inside of those nightclubs and bars see many DJ's come and they've seen many DJ's go. You definitely want to be grateful for the opportunity to express your talent. Nowadays there's a huge problem where a lot of guys expect to play for hundreds but they've never played for a dead bar or a dead venue. Always be humble, when you fall from grace which often happens then those people below you will either push you down or help you back up.

How to Read a Crowd

Before you play out at any venue you need to understand what kind of crowd is going to be there and what taste of music they're into. Is it a young crowd? Is it an old crowd? Is it a ravy crowd? Is it a VIP crowd? There's all sorts of different crowds where you need to cater to but even playing from country to country it can be different. For instance trap is big in USA but not so much in the UK. In Brazil they like anything that has to do with Samba or like tribal drum orientated. You can start out with research, look up the venue and who has played there. Ask the owners and staff. Prepare your set in accordance. If you don't have the luxury of that then here are some tools you can use when you are mixing.

First of all arrive early and take a walk around the venue. Check out what kind of customers are there. Young, old, female, European, etc. Listen to what the DJ before you plays and observe how the crowd reacts. Feel the energy and the vibe, is the crowd really engaged or are they on their phones or are they walking on and off the dancefloor? It's important to take a mental note of this before you jump on because you need to really understand if you need to take up your set a level or perhaps bring it down. If you are headlining and have the chance to talk with the warm up DJ then let them know what kind of style you will be playing. Of course you don't want to play the same songs. If your the warm up DJ then be aware of the songs or genres to avoid and don't play too hard. Save that for the main act. You might be the first DJ on and no one's dancing. But if they look like they're having a good time the odds are that they're just really enjoying your set but aren't ready to dance yet.

When you are playing you want to keep the center of the dance floor packed and moving. If you have an empty dance floor then the crowd is not engaging anymore and you need to switch it up. Pay attention and watch the faces of the crowd so that you can still see if people are happy. Read their body language, watch for minor body movement like smiles, tapping at one's feet or nodding heads. You must also be engaged and be part of the party. Feel the music, don't be the guy that's separated from the party. Be together with the crowd, you make the party and if you feel like dancing then it's most likely the crowd will also feel like dancing.

When trying to read a room you can go all directions with it. You can give them more, you can give them less and if you give them less purposely then you can always come back with more. But at a certain point you'll lose your momentum and momentum is what it's all about. Creating the right moments, the right build ups and not just in one track but a storyline that you're trying to tell through your DJ set. Sometimes you could have a diverse crowd for example with pockets of high energy people, pockets of people liking hits, pockets of people liking underground stuff or new stuff or classics. Make sure your really flexible to keep catering to the crowd in any given situation. If you have a commercial crowd make sure you play something by DJ Snake or The Chainsmokers or whatever is hot now. If you have an underground crowd make sure to give them plenty of stuff they don't know. If you have a young crowd go for that festival vibe, play those EDM bangers, trap and dubstep. If you have an older crowd make sure you keep it housey and you can play plenty of throwbacks.

Reading a crowd is perhaps one of the hardest things to do as a DJ. If you can pull it off it will help you get more gigs in return. When you're in a nightclub you've got to be mindful of building energy in the night and not overstepping other DJ's. When people rock into a club the reality is that they just don't want to dance for the first hour or two. Normally they want to wait for someone to break the ice and make the first move. So if no one's dancing yet it's often a good idea to play to the women as they normally are the first ones to dance and then the boys will follow. The main aim is to keep the crowd happy no matter where you're playing. Being a club DJ you should be more about educating the crowd. Of course your often playing familiar songs to an extent but bringing your own representation of style and your music tastes to the table. Not just playing top ten hits, but really pushing the boundaries. However as a wedding or a function DJ you're just purely playing popular music because usually people there will only really recognize popular music.

Working with an MC

Some clubs often have a resident MC and their job is to hype up the crowd. It's great if you can have someone work with you who knows your style. I have worked with the same MC for years and you end up developing a great rapport. If it's someone new, make sure you have time to chat with them first. Share music and what your set ideas are so that you can gel and understand each other. You need to be in harmony with that person. If you are working alone then you might need to MC. But don't worry it doesn't require having an amazing, booming voice. Most crowds are drunk and all you need to do is a hype them up a little bit. Put your hands up, are you ready, make some noise! These are all good go to, things to say. Before you speak into the microphone make sure you warm up your voice. You don't want to sound all hoarse and croaky. Use some basic vocal warm up exercises such as humming or ahhhs.

Dealing With Nerves

Your about to go on stage. Your hands are shaking, your throat is dry and your mind is blank. How the hell can you perform like this? Calm down. The first step to avoiding nerves is preparation. If you are well prepared and practiced then your confidence will be higher. There should be no holes in your set. Make sure you have a good idea of the place your playing and sound check if it's possible before. If you still feel nervous then realize that nerves are simply trapped energy. This might seem like a ridiculous thing to do but movement will release that tension. Jump, stretch, shout, pound your chest and get rid of that energy. Visualize your success and enjoy the moment. Remember that music is fun and you should smile, dance and enjoy it. This will be infectious to your audience. If you feel it, they feel it.

The key to all of this is confidence and you can always fake it until you make it. The one who believes in themselves the most leads and that is your job as a DJ, to lead.

Good luck!

FAQ and Top Tips

How do I deal with song requests?

Normally I would avoid requests unless they fit with your set. When someone asks your for a song, just say yes. Then they will go away and usually forget. Or say sorry I don't have it. If they are obnoxious, give security the nod.

How do I get the crowd pumped?

The obvious answer is to go commercial or mix in some classics. Usually people lose interest if the music is too new. You might also be playing too slow or too hard. Just think what is the opposite and try that route until you get more interaction.

What happens if my USB fails?

Always keep a back up. Whenever you export, do it twice to two USB drives.

How can I get more bookings?

Get out there and meet people. Add value, create content and share it. Increase your visibility by boosting your posts. Contact clubs and follow up.

How can I improve?

Practice makes perfect. Get a mentor and ask them for feedback. Record your mixes and listen back.

Where can I get mashups?

www.soundcloud.com www.hypeedit.com
DJ City
Or make your own.

What gear do I need to start?

A controller, laptop, software, speakers and headphones.

What if the warm up DJ is playing to hard?

Tell them manager or politely tell them yourself.

What if I trainwreck a mix?

Try to disguise it with effects and move on quickly. Practice makes perfect. If you have new music, test it at home first.

What if a club doesn't reply?

Follow up twice and then move on.

How do I score a hot chick?

Print business cards or have your friend go talk with them.

Should I drink?

I would not recommend it. But if customers insist then pretend to.

Am I too old or too young?

It depends where you play. Most clubs have an age limit of 18 or 20 and up. Your never too old, as long as you have energy. David Guetta is fifty plus and Carl Cox is almost sixty. Both icons.

Do I need to produce my own music?

You can easily get local gigs through hustling. Producing helps get you on a global stage. But if you are great at marketing or hustling then you can still get booked. Alternatively you can pay a ghost producer to make some hits for you.

About The Author

DJ Swindali has fast established himself as one of the hottest names on the touring circuit.

With new artists appearing every day, it takes nothing short of raw talent to stand out.

Born in England he drew on the country's rich heritage in dance music and began his rise to success sharing the stage with international DJs including, Chase and Status, Fatboy Slim, Goldie, High Contrast and more. In a natural evolution, he began producing music and was awarded a First Class Honors Degree in Music, was featured on BBC Radio 1 emerging talents and also set up his own record label to be distributed by Sony.

Inspired by the scene in Asia he relocated there five years ago. In this short space of time he has quickly made a name for himself, holding residencies at world famous nightclubs including his current residency at two of the top clubs in Bangkok, Route 66 and Insanity.

Major labels have taken notice of his music productions. Live Nation recently signed his collaboration with Ozmo on the hit song "Still Here", and "Overdose" with the famous singer Donyale Rene. Multiple times he has hit the Beatport Top 100 charts, has generated over 100,000 plays on SoundCloud and was rewarded three top ten's plus a number one mix on Mixcloud. All whilst growing a worldwide fanbase with over six thousand fans on Facebook, over fifteen thousand on Instagram and more counting.

Demand for DJ Swindali has seen him headline multiple music festivals, perform live on Fashion TV and conquer several famous venues, including Illuzion in Thailand, Sir Teen in Beijing, and several noteworthy appearances throughout the rest of the world. Including Shanghai, Malaysia, Taipei, Hong Kong, Cambodia, Oman, Myanmar, Japan, Vietnam and more to come.

For more information

www.swindali.com

Thanks for Reading!

What did you think of, **Music Production & DJing for EDM: Everything You Need To Know To Become A World Famous EDM DJ & Music Producer**

I know you could have picked any number of books to read, but you picked this book and for that I am extremely grateful.

I hope that it added at value and quality to your everyday life. If so, it would be really nice if you could share this book with your friends and family by posting to [Facebook](#) and [Twitter](#).

If you enjoyed this book and found some benefit in reading this, I'd like to hear from you and hope that you could take some time to post a review. Your feedback and support will help this author to greatly improve his writing craft for future projects and make this book even better.

I want you, the reader, to know that your review is very important and so, if you'd like to leave a review, all you have to do is click here and away you go. I wish you all the best in your future success!

Also check out my other books:

[Music Production: Everything You Need To Know About Producing Music and Songwriting](#)

[Music Production: How to Produce Music, The Easy to Read Guide for Music Producers Introduction](#)

Songwriting: Apply Proven Methods, Ideas and Exercises to Kickstart or Upgrade Your Songwriting

Thank you and good luck!

Tommy Swindali
2019

Discover "Top DJ Tips & FAQ" Cheat Sheet

http://howtodj.ontrapages.com/

DJ Swindali Music Coaching/Skype Lessons.

Email djswindali@gmail.com for info and pricing

Claim This Now

Music Business Skills for Musicians:

If you're in the music business, read on. Today you need to view yourself through the new rules of the music industry.

Those who play by them will succeed.

Gone are the old days where you would hope to get signed and then become a star (i.e., everything would be done for you).

Do you wonder why other artists are getting breaks and you are not?

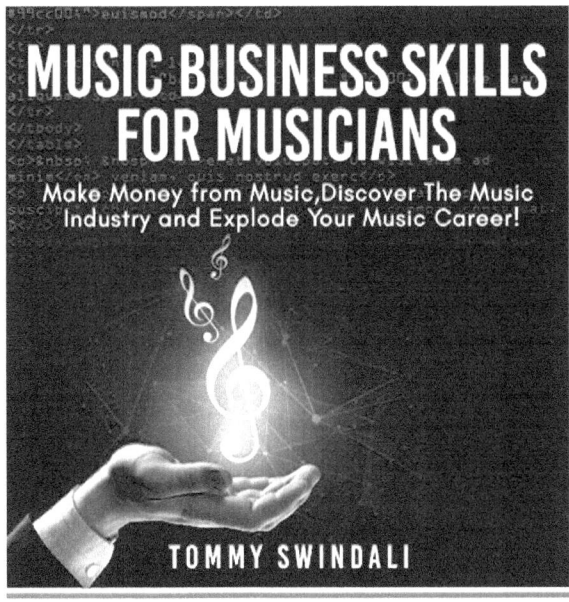

Discover How To Find Your Sound

Find Out More

Swindali music coaching/Skype lessons.

Email djswindali@gmail.com for info and pricing.

Other Books by Tommy Swindali

In The Mix: Discover The Secrets to Becoming a Successful DJ

If you have ever dreamed of being a DJ with people dancing to your music and all whilst having the time of your life then this book will show you how. Find Out More

Music Production: The Advanced Guide On How to Produce for Music Producers

Learn to Produce Music Like a Pro and Take Your Music To a Whole New Level Find Out More

Music Business Skills For Musicians
If Your In The Music Business, Read On Today you need to view yourself through the new rules of the music industry. Those who play by them will succeed Find Out More

Songwriting: Apply Proven Methods, Ideas and Exercises to Kickstart or Upgrade Your Songwriting

Have you ever listened to a song and thought "wow, if only I could write a song like that"? Well, you can now learn all the secrets on how to write beautiful music with this guide to songwriting! Find Out More

www.ingramcontent.com/pod-product-compliance
Lightning Source LLC
Chambersburg PA
CBHW021108080526
44587CB00010B/433